MK 43 e₁

OLD MOORE'S

HOROSCOPE
AND ASTRAL
DIARY

•

GEMINI

GW00501803

foulsham
LONDON • NEW YORK • TORONTO • SYDNEY

foulsham

Yeovil Road, Slough, Berkshire, SL1 4JH

ISBN 0-572-01735-9

Copyright © 1992 W. Foulsham & Co. Ltd.

Printed in Great Britain by Cox & Wyman Ltd., Reading.

CONTENTS

OLD MOORE'S HOROSCOPE AND ASTRAL DIARY

Old Moore's Horoscope and Astral Diary represents a major departure from the usual format of publications dedicated to popular Sun-sign astrology. In this book, more attention than ever before has been focused on the discovery of the 'real you', through a wealth of astrological information, presented in an easy to follow and interesting form, and designed to provide a comprehensive insight into your fundamental nature.

The interplay of the Sun and Moon form complex cycles that are brought to bear on each of us in different ways. In the pages that follow I will explain how a knowledge of these patterns in your life can make relationships with others easier and general success more possible. Realising when your mind and body are at their most active or inactive, and at what times your greatest efforts are liable to see you winning through, can be of tremendous importance. In addition, your interaction with other zodiac types is explored, together with a comprehensive explanation of your Sun-sign nature,

In the Astral Diary you will discover a day-to-day reading covering a fifteen-month period. The readings are compiled from solar, lunar and planetary relationships as they bear upon your own zodiac sign. In addition, easy-to-follow graphic charts offer you at a glance an understanding of the way that your personal life-cycles are running; what days are best for maximum effort and when your system is likely to be regenerating.

Because some people want to look deeper into the fascinating world of personal astrology, there is a section of the book allowing a more in-depth appraisal of the all-important zodiac sign that was 'Rising' at the time of your birth and another showing what bearing your 'Descending' sign has on relationships. Beyond this you can learn about the very real part that the Moon has to play in your life.,

From a simple-to-follow diary section, on to an intimate understanding of the ever-changing child of the solar system that you are, my Horoscope and Astral Diary will allow you to unlock potential that you never even suspected you had.

With the help and guidance of the following pages, Old Moore wishes you a happy and prosperous future.

HERE'S LOOKING AT YOU

A ZODIAC PORTRAIT OF GEMINI
(22nd MAY - 21st JUNE)

Most astrological descriptions of the physical attributes of Gemini make reference to the Twins' youthful appearance and it is very true that, if you are as old as you feel, then those people born under the influence of Gemini can remain young and vital, almost to any age. In terms of physical appearance, the Mercury ruled Gemini subject is often slim to medium in build, with a quick active walk and a recognisable urgency in every movement that they make. Add to this sparkling eyes, a mischievous grin and a razor sharp intellect housed within that noble head and there you have it, probably the most enigmatic and certainly the most communicative sign of the zodiac - Gemini

Of course, in terms of your actual appearance, much also depends on the zodiac sign that was climbing over the eastern horizon at the time of your birth but, more often than not, Geminis also sport an oval face, darkish complexion and a clear skin. The active frame comes as a result of surviving on the abundant store of nervous energy that so typifies your sign. You live on 'the edge' most of the time and can be more susceptible to minor health problems as a result. At times of extreme stress, or when you have expected too much of yourself for a protracted period, it is in the regions of your shoulders, arms, chest and of course that vulnerable nervous system that problems can arise. You need to be active most of the time to stay happy, can be irritable if crossed but are never, ever boring to have around.

THE INTENTION

The motivating factors under-pinning your oh so complex nature are not at all easy to fathom, though amongst the obvious character traits that come gift-wrapped to almost any Gemini at birth is an insatiable curiosity, which makes you a sponge when it comes to picking up information from your environment. You need a clear and concise picture of the universe of which you are part, even if your methods of gaining the knowledge could appear to be somewhat haphazard when observed by less dynamic, more ordered signs. Most noticeable of all is your duality of nature - the zodiac sign of Gemini is the Twins after all! One of these celestial partners is often quite logical, assimilating information meticulously and aware of the need for scientific appraisal, whilst the other is invariably working on a more intuitive level; a dreamy type who seeks to synthesise the mysteries of a complex and fascinating world into one serene and fathomable whole. Here is the fascination of the Gemini, but also the enigma.

Having set out on your path to understand what makes the world go round, the next most important action is to communicate the fact to anyone and everyone that you come across. With a lightning intellect and a razor sharp wit, you set out to charm, and at the same time disarm, a breathless and unsuspecting public. You can talk on almost any subject under the sun, even ones that you probably know little or nothing about, have an ability to parody and mimic and may be equally good at communicating your ideas via the written word. You are the mental gymnast, whose irresistible desire to 'know' can lead you into more adventures in a year than many people would experience in a lifetime.

YOUR VIRTUES

Most Gemini subjects are sympathetic and kind-hearted, which taken together with your ability to keep people amused, assures you of many friendships in your life. It is true that you will have an equal amount of acquaintances, people who are not particularly important to you, and some astrologers have been unkind to Gemini on this score, accusing the sign of being naturally unfaithful. Generally speaking this is not true for Geminis invariably make staunch and loyal allies.

In any emergency you can be relied upon to act quickly and well, because your mind goes into hyper-drive at such times and the first concern is always for the person who may be in some sort of trouble or danger. As nature's experimenter and investigator, you reason things out that would baffle a university professor and enjoy being basically mysterious, despite the fact that you tell the whole world that you have nothing at all to hide. Keeping busy is important to you, likewise having more than one iron in the fire. Of course you will come across a fair cross-section of people who don't take to you, which can bruise your surprisingly vulnerable ego, but you revel in the love of the hundreds of individuals who find you good to have around and you would do anything to make the people that you love happy. Changeable and inspiring, you are at the head of anything that takes your fancy, can be dexterous and skilful and leave an air of cheerful optimism behind you wherever you choose to wander. Travel is important to you because it broadens your horizons and you get on especially well with people from different cultures and backgrounds. Although it is possible for the average Gemini to argue the hind-leg off a donkey, you rarely bear a grudge and usually take reversals in your stride.

YOUR VICES

There is little doubt that those born under the influence of the Twins can be very aggravating on occasions. In fairness to you this may be partly because you are usually correct in your assumptions, though you are not always as sensitive to the other person's point of view as you could be and can land yourself in hot water as a result. Exuding an air of superficiality, the average Gemini is inclined to skim the surface of life, failing to notice the undercurrents that play beneath. On occasions this will incline you to be somewhat cruel to others, albeit unintentionally. Is it a lack of emotional depth that makes you inclined to walk on the sensitivity of others? Almost certainly not; the problem seems to be that your busy, busy schedule doesn't always allow you the time to think before you speak - probably your worst fault. On the other hand, once your enthusiasm is raised, you can be of tremendous help to other people and a tireless worker on behalf of mankind as a whole. Whatever you become involved in, you need a ranging brief and work at your best when allowed to use your own intuition. Intellectually motivated, you are generally beyond the concepts of class or creed divisions and probably care very much about third world and ecology issues. Geminis are usually well ahead of their time and need to pick the bones out of everything that they come across in life, but can be a bore if others don't follow their quick thinking and impossibly reforming zeal.

Although you are quite willing to analyse anyone and everyone, you don't always look too deeply into your own motivations at the start of any project. As a result you often stop a particular action in mid-stream, having discovered that it is not really for you. This would be fine if the situation only affected your own life, but so often you leave others stranded out of their depth, whilst you happily turn your vacillating mind elsewhere.

'Love them and leave them' typifies the worst romantic excesses of your sign, though most Mercurial sons and daughters fall short of this most unfortunate extreme; nevertheless, you may well have more than one attachment in your life. On occasions you can also be accused of being rather liberal with the truth, after all Mercury is the patron god of liars, cheats and con-men in addition to his more acceptable guardianship of speakers and messengers. Restless, changeable and fickle; too easily bored by conventions and as noisy as a chattering monkey. So say your critics - but then you are never that sort of person at all, are you?

LIVING A HAPPY LIFE

Because you expect so much of yourself, it is very important for you to take time out to relax and to meditate. Your work should be stimulating and offer the sort of variety that makes your mentally motivated nature sing with joy, in which case your career becomes nothing more than an extension of your adventure through life. Too much pressure really isn't good for the Gemini subject, no matter how indestructible they may consider themselves to be. Nervous fatigue is your worst potential enemy and can lead to other health problems if it remains unchecked.

In any sort of partnership you need to aware that the people you are dealing with are able to get their own point of view across, and this is just as important in a working environment as it would be in a more intimate relationship. It isn't that you mean to be overbearing, it's just that you are so good at expressing yourself, less talkative types sometimes don't always get a look in. No matter how you feel at the time, it isn't good for the Gemini to get all his or her own way, and you achieve a much happier life when you really learn to share.

Food intake also needs to be carefully monitored, allowing for a mixture of speed (you never have time to hang around) and nutrition. You need to be needed, and so a secure and comfortable personal life really does suit you the best. But far and away the most important factor of all is that you must be happy, for the deflated, defeated Gemini is like a wild, free bird condemned to live its life behind the bars of a cramped and soul-destroying cage.

WHAT'S RISING ?

YOUR RISING SIGN AND PERSONALITY

Perhaps you have come across this term 'Rising Sign' when looking at other books on astrology and may have been somewhat puzzled as to what it actually means. To those not accustomed to astrological jargon it could sound somewhat technical and mysterious, though in fact, in terms of your own personal birth chart, it couldn't be simpler. The Rising Sign is simply that part of the zodiac occupying the eastern horizon at the time of your birth. Because it is a little more difficult to discover than your Sun-sign, many writers of popular astrology have tended to ignore it, which is a great shame, because, together with the Sun, your Rising Sign is the single most important factor in terms of setting your personality. So much so, that no appraisal of your astrological nature could be complete without it.

Your Rising Sign, also known as your 'Ascendant' or 'Ascending Sign' plays a great part in your looks - yes, astrology can even predict what you are going to be like physically. In fact, this is a very interesting point, because there appears to be a tie-in between astrology and genetics. Professional astrologers for centuries have noted the close relationship that often exists between the astrological birth chart of parents and those of their offspring, so that, if you look like your Mother or Father, chances are that there is a close astrological tie. Rising Signs especially appear to be handed down through families.

The first impression that you get, in an astrological sense, upon meeting a stranger, is not related to their Sun-sign but to the zodiac sign that was rising at the moment they came into the world. The Rising Sign is particularly important because it modifies the way that you display your Sun-sign to the world at large. A good example of this might be that of Britain's best known ex-Primeminister, Margaret Thatcher. This dynamic and powerful lady is a Libran by Sun-sign placing, indicating a light-hearted nature, pleasure loving and very flexible. However, Mrs Thatcher has Scorpio as her Rising Sign, bringing a steely determination and a tremendous capacity for work. It also bestows an iron will and the power to thrive under pressure.

Here lies the true importance of the Rising Sign, for Mr Thatcher almost certainly knows a woman who most other people do not. The Rising Sign is a protective shell, and not until we know someone quite well do we start to discover the Sun-sign nature that hides within this often tough outer coat of astrological making. Your Rising Sign also represents your basic self-image, the social mask that is often so useful; and even if you don't think that you conform to the interpretation of your Ascendant, chances are that other people will think that you do.

Not only an individual's looks are down to the Rising Sign, but also the way they walk, sit and generally present themselves to the world. For example, a person possessed of Gemini Rising is apt to be very quick, energetic in all movements, deliberate in mannerisms and with a cheerful disposition. A bearer of a Taurean Ascendant on the other hand would probably not be so tall, more solid generally, quieter in aspect and calmer in movement. Once you come to understand the basics of astrology it is really very easy to pick out the Rising Signs of people that you come across, even though the Sun-sign is often more difficult to pin down. Keep an eye open for the dynamic and positive Aries Rising individual, or the retiring, shy but absolutely magnetic quality of of the Piscean Ascendant. Of course, in astrology, nothing is quite that simple. The position of a vast array of heavenly bodies at the time of birth also has to be taken into account, particularly that of the Moon and the inner planets Mercury and Venus. Nevertheless a knowledge of the Rising Sign can be an invaluable aid in getting to know what really makes any person tick as an individual.

To ascertain the exact degree of your Rising Sign takes a little experience and recourse to some special material. However, I have evolved a series of tables that will enable you to discover at a glance what your Rising Sign is likely to be. All you need to know is the approximate time of your birth. At the back of the book you will find the necessary table related to your Sun-sign. Simply look down the left-hand column until you find your approximate time of birth, am or pm. Now scan across the top of the table to the place where your date of birth is shown. Look for the square where the two pieces of information connect and there is your Rising Sign. Once you know what your Rising Sign is, read on, and learn even more about the fascinating interplay of astrological relationship.

GEMINI WITH GEMINI RISING

If anything is going to make you display yourself to the world at large as a typical Gemini should, the position of your Sun in the Rising Sign will do so. Having Gemini as your Sun-sign and Rising Sign too means that you were born at or near to dawn. Here is a powerful nature indeed, since all the exuberance and dynamism bestowed by the Twins is inherent in your nature. You are likely to be a very good talker, dexterous and imaginative. Life is a game to you and one that can be as fascinating as any adventure story. Few people can resist the force of your charm, or that silver tongue, that can get you in and out of the most unbelievable scrapes on occasions.

Although you are quick-tempered you calm down again just as rapidly. Confidence is something that you appear to have in abundance, though you may not be half as secure underneath as you like to give the impression of being. You need a job that allows you to use your mental dexterity and a life that presents the sort of freedom that is meat and drink to any Gemini, and especially one who has a double dose of the Mercurial magic.

GEMINI WITH CANCER RISING

You don't appear at first sight to have a great deal in common with your Sun-sign of Gemini, particularly since you are inclined to cloud the generally clear-minded qualities of the Twins with all manner of sentimental considerations. On many occasions it is true that your feelings, ever the domain of deep Cancer, cloud your instinctive judgements and as a result it is natural that others should try to dupe you, considering that you may be a soft touch.

On the positive side, you have a fondness for home and family, and an ability to approach them on equal terms. Your caring instincts are finely tuned and you are more than capable of protecting yourself, not to mention the other intimates who form such an important part of your life. Moods are deeper and longer lasting than would the the case with the typical Gemini and you have a reclusive quality that contradicts your more social Gemini instincts quite noticeably. At heart you are easy-going though, if a little reticent to allow certain people into the private shell that the 'crabby' side of your nature is inclined to build around the gregarious Twins. You have the ability to make other people happy and to provide a sound and happy base from which to operate.

GEMINI WITH LEO RISING

This is the perfect combination for a salesperson because here the gift of the gab balances with the determination to succeed and the sunny disposition of the Lion. In social contact there is nobody to touch you, though it would be very surprising if you have never been accused of being overbearing on occasions - that is if anyone is brave enough to make such a suggestion. Some of the pride and the 'snobbery' that are seen as negative traits in the case of Leo are probably missing from your nature, eradicated by the more egalitarian quality of the Twins.

Others think well of you, your friends are honest and their care for you is apt to endure. You have more constancy and staying -power than would be expected from Gemini alone, and yet all the ability to overcome obstacles and force your way to the top of any pile that you choose. Beware only of a stubborn streak, so deep set in your nature that only half a lifetime of practising flexibility could eradicate it. Opt instead for the breezy flexibility of Gemini, a fine compliment to the high-minded realms of Leo.

GEMINI WITH VIRGO RISING

Both Gemini and Virgo are ruled by the planet Mercury, though he shows a radically different face to the deep, earthy recesses of Virgo than his more benign smile in Gemini. Nevertheless, the chatty side of your Gemini nature still shows, even if it is underpinned by a certain indefinable reserve and the hint of a nature deeper than a bottomless well. You may accuse yourself of failing to really understand others on an inner level, yet your intuition is such that the only critic you would find on this score is likely to be yourself. You really don't have all that much self confidence, despite the fact that your 'shallowness' is a figment of your own imagination.

The thing to learn here is that too much intellectualising is not at all a good thing. What you have to do now is to learn how to love yourself in a world full of people who all appear to have more to offer than you do, and yet at the same time avoid an apparent smugness that can infuriate others. This is no easy task, though you should find it to be worth the effort in terms of popularity. Communication has to be the key here and you are a talker beyond every other consideration, though you must listen too.

GEMINI WITH LIBRA RISING

There is no doubt that you were born under a wandering star, for both Gemini and Libra are 'Air signs', increasing the inquisitive qualities of your nature and making it vital for you to be constantly searching for answers to a million questions that beset you. Full of the charm that so typifies the sign of Libra, and which is also to be seen in Gemini when at its best, you are, nevertheless, something of a social butterfly. You undoubtedly have many cultured friends who enable you to retain your basic assertion that the world is a place of harmony and beauty, and can be disappointed when you realise that often it isn't.

Most Libran Geminis enjoy travelling, are delightful and witty companions and can always be relied upon to spin a good 'yarn' guaranteed to entertain the many and varied ranks of people they meet on their journey through life. It is fair to say that you often deal in superficialities, don't really like to get your hands dirty. except in the garden, and prefer the company of people who share your view of the world.

GEMINI WITH SCORPIO RISING

Scorpio can indeed be a 'heavy' Rising Sign, for it is penetrating and deep. Nevertheless, you almost certainly retain much of the chatty informality of your Gemini Sun, a smoke-screen dreamed up by that powerful Rising Sign, designed to fool the world into thinking that you are some kind of Bertie Wooster. Nothing could be further from the truth. Your insights are penetrating and you possess an almost irrational intensity that only the lucky few are ever likely to see. Whether you are being creative or philosophical you always have something vital to say and of course nobody would dream of wandering off whilst you are doing so.

Like all people with Scorpio ascending, you care very deeply about the things that you see as being personally important, are tremendously loyal to your friends and probably show an intense interest in the occult. Mystery in all its forms appeals to you, though who would guess, when you hide so well behind that happy-go-lucky exterior. It is not an intensity shown to the world at large that needs to be looked at carefully - but that which hides so deeply within your own nature. You can often retreat into the more sensuous qualities of your Scorpio side but always keep one foot in the real world.

GEMINI WITH SAGITTARIUS RISING

You really are life's eternal optimist, and it isn't that you live a life of unique privilege either, being just as susceptible to ups and downs as any other type of Gemini. What really sets you apart is your overwhelming belief in a brighter tomorrow, which of course makes you very popular to have around and only very occasionally nauseating if you take this sunny attitude too far. Of course, there is a negative side to everything and in your case it is your inability to come to terms with much in the way of responsibility. The truth is that you are a bit of a gypsy, quite willing to look out for yourself but not too keen on saving the world from its own folly. It's a 'live and let live' attitude, sometimes carried too far.

You have much to say for yourself, indeed you can be very outspoken, and your sense of humour is almost legendary. But what goes on in the recesses of that jovial mind, and how much personal pain does it sometimes mask? We will never know, because like many Geminis you talk much - but say little.

GEMINI WITH CAPRICORN RISING

Like all people with Capricorn contacts, what you are really looking for in life is security, and your keen, shrewd eye often allows you the chance to get right to the top of the pile in your search for it. Underlying the bright and cheerful exterior is a keen intellect, honed to perfection by experience, cool and methodical and always watching what is going on in your vicinity.

Like all Geminis. you exhibit wit and a keen sense of humour, though unlike some of the others you are inclined to put your sense of duty above what could be considered to be more important qualities, and may lose some of the gloss from life as a result. In relationships you have more sincerity than most but you can fret terribly if ill-health gets in the way, or on those occasions that you feel life is not doing all it might to further your interests. Basically, you believe that you were put on earth to achieve a state of perfection, a fact that is quite sensible when viewed from your side of the fence, but one which might not be so easy for others to come to terms with. People with this combination have the ability to sort out the most complicated of muddles, either in a personal or in a practical sense. You should have plenty of friends, but could find compliments hard to take.

GEMINI WITH AQUARIUS RISING

Like all individuals who have a strong Aquarian content to their birth charts, you are seen by the world as being decidedly unconventional. When the Air signs of the Twins and the Water Bearer come together as they do here, the natural inventiveness of Gemini goes out through the roof, sometimes appearing to create a distinctly 'eccentric' personality, though one that is very attractive to others. Whilst on the one hand you must be a member of a group to feel comfortable, at the same time intuitive foresight tells you that the individual in you cannot be compromised - no wonder you are often at odds with yourself.

Being very creative, you are a true original in every sense of the world, love life to the full and rarely find yourself stuck for something to say. When it comes to collecting information, nothing is beneath your dignity or your insatiable thirst for knowledge, yet there is a quite easily perceived coolness and an authority that makes the whole world trust your judgement. Intimacy can be a problem and in relationships an intellectual meeting of souls is just as important as any physical attraction.

GEMINI WITH PISCES RISING

Two Twins - two fishes, some say a recipe for chaos. An understandable observation when you look at the duality inherent in both these zodiac signs. There is an inconsistency here that is almost impossible for you to come to terms with, let alone an unsuspecting world that must deal with you. You have to avoid self-pity at all costs, and once you have eradicated this worst of all possible faults from your nature, there is little in you to dislike. The sympathy that you show to practically everyone that you meet makes you appear at times to be a living saint, which is why you are definitely at your best when you are giving and not getting. Being in touch with your own inner self is possible, whereas it definitely isn't with other Gemini clones. But how to make the most of this formidable combination and rise in your own estimation too? Not easy perhaps, but remember this. You are generous, charitable, warm and extremely loving. The whole world is your friend and you don't bear grudges. In a world full of people who are longing to be loved, what more could anyone ask? You need to stay away from a confusing or complicated personal life and would be at your best in a known and trusted relationship.

GEMINI WITH ARIES RISING

Let's get your worst potential fault out of the way before we go any further. Quite bluntly, you never stop talking! There are times when this can be a good thing and no doubt you can lift your life as a result of your gift of the gab, but remember, you dear, lovable rogue, that there is beauty in silence too. To make up for any deficiency implied here, you are frank and candid in a way that any Gemini mistruster would find to be extremely refreshing. At the same time you have a hatred for conventions, especially 'stuffy ones' and can be guaranteed to cock-a-snook at orthodoxy wherever you meet it. For this aspect of your nature you are loved; being everything that most other people want to be but dare not.

You are quick off the mark where temper is concerned, though you calm down just as quickly and never bear a grudge. Perhaps most important of all is the ability you have to use your flashes of inspiration to see clean through to the heart of any situation - or person come to that!

GEMINI WITH TAURUS RISING

When the lightning quick reactions of Gemini induce greater reaction into the often too careful Taurean plodder, or the methodical Bull demands greater attention from the capricious Twins, all is well. All too often your life is a system of stop-start, because, like oil and water, it's hard to get a satisfactory mix of these two radically different zodiac types. Despite this possibility, you are easy going, very creative and can make speech flow like warm honey. You ought to try your hand at writing - especially poetry, for you have the power to coax tears and laughter from the same stanza. Not that you are totally abstract in your approach to life. There is plenty of money to be made if you turn your mind to doing so, and since you like the good things is life you probably will. You have tenacity enough to see any project through to the end and will still be working when all the other Geminis are out at the disco. Look to the wealth of ideas that inhabit that fertile imagination; incorporate them into your basic love of others and make them work for you. Look for the practical aspects of life and concentrate on them because you are both creative and capable. With the sort of good, lasting friends that you make, and a partner to share the perfect world you create, happiness is certain to follow.

WHAT'S DESCENDING

YOUR DESCENDING SIGN AND RELATIONSHIPS

If the term 'Rising Sign' is largely ignored in popular astrology, the 'Descendant' is utilised even less, despite the fact that it has much to say about the basic nature of any individual. Once you know what your Rising Sign is, the Descending Sign is easy to discover, since it represents the opposite zodiac sign to that which was Rising at your birth. To discover which sign is opposite to your own Rising Sign look through the following section. At the head of each reading you can see the appropriate Rising Sign in brackets. If, for example, you were born with Taurus Rising, you will see that this is listed along with the Scorpio Descendant. This is the section that would apply specifically to you.

Whereas the Rising Sign shows the mask that we wear in our everyday life, our Descending Sign relates to what we see as our 'opposite' self reflected in others, and perhaps the qualities that we do our best to draw from them in terms of compensation. This works to a greater or lesser degree in all our interactions with other people - whether we realise the fact or not.

It isn't so surprising then that the seventh house, that part of an astrological birth chart that is traditionally associated with the Descendant, is the place that astrologers look to discover the possible nature of the marriage partner. However, the seventh house doesn't disclose what a person's life partner will actually be like, more what we as individuals try to derive from them in order to compensate for our own shortcomings; faults and failings that are indicated by the Descendant's position.

Since the Descendant shows what we strive to attract in terms of parts of ourselves that are incomplete or need work, we could do far worse than to take a look at our make-up in its light. By so doing we may glimpse a side of ourselves that can all too easily be lost in a desire to observe only the positive aspects of our nature. After all, the position of our Sun and Ascendant speak about what we 'have', whereas the Descendant can tell us what we 'need'.

ARIES DESCENDANT (LIBRA RISING)

It is quite often your mild-mannered, reasonable and diplomatic approach to the whole of life that draws certain self-assertive, even objectionable people into your personal world. If you are surprised at this, then consider the principle of the attraction of opposites: your relationships often have precisely the kind of quality you seek to avoid, usually because you are too 'nice' to people. However, what drives you inwardly is the search for a partner who is a dynamic individualist, someone who will stand up and be counted, a pioneer and an enthusiast. If such qualities are not developed within yourself, then you can expect them to surface in your close relationships. It is only to be hoped that you like what you find.

TAURUS DESCENDANT (SCORPIO RISING)

Complementing your 'I don't give a damn' exterior is the inward need to enjoy the closeness and security of a loving and caring relationship. However much you may strike outsiders as being intense and powerful, your partner is well aware that this is merely a mask concealing your inner softness and vulnerability in close relationships. There is a deep desire to form a relationship that will endure, containing lasting value and be solid and permanent. Even if you reject such notions of security, perhaps because they smack of something boring and 'samey', you will attract such a situation through a partner, simply because it is what you ultimately want, or at the very least what you instinctively need.

GEMINI DESCENDANT (SAGITTARIUS RISING)

Your broad-minded tolerance, generous spirit, and ultimately positive nature are of course qualities to be admired. However, this expansiveness of yours often has an unfortunate side-effect: your feet keep leaving the ground and off you fly into the lofty world of ideals once more. What you are ultimately looking for, and will find, is someone who can remind you of the finite details of the here and now; in short, an individual to keep your feet on solid ground. Of course, you are bored with petty details and someone who reminds you of what-is-what, yet this is something that you will continually encounter until you can appreciate the so-called art of the small for its own sake.

CANCER DESCENDANT (CAPRICORN RISING)

With your utterly conservative and often over-serious way of dealing with life (where everything must be realistic) it may surprise you to know that you are inwardly trying to come to terms with the more fluid and sensitive aspects of your nature, where practical realism plays no part whatsoever. And it is in the arena of close partnerships that you find this more ambiguous and emotional side to yourself. You will often discover a kind of maternal aspect in the person with whom you share your life. the one who worries about making certain that you are eating properly - that sort of thing. However, this is not the kind of situation that bothers you. It's all of those insipid emotions that puzzle you. Perhaps one day you will discover what really makes you tick!

LEO DESCENDANT (AQUARIUS RISING)

It is a widely held and quite admirable belief that we are all brothers and sisters under the skin, that we are all ultimately equal and should work together in society towards the common good - so why doesn't your partner see things in quite this way? You attract many people who believe that some individuals are in reality more equal than others, and that to be the best in one's field it is a waste of time looking over your shoulder whilst scheming your way to the top. Such notions are quite abhorrent to you, yet you often attract types who could easily be labelled as selfish, demanding, overbearing and big-headed, even though, to you, nobody is particularly special.

VIRGO DESCENDANT (PISCES RISING)

Now let me guess; your life is a constant fight against chaos, emotional turbulence and things which simply go wrong. But there is often some guardian angel to pull you out when things get too hairy, and you can find the discipline inside yourself to untangle the mess. That's the Virgo inside you, and it is ultimately the well-disciplined type to whom you gravitate, someone whose capability in the sphere of material concerns is second to none. You attract the helpful sort, of course, in your relationships, yet you must not mind if you find them to be a wee bit critical of your faults: impractical, vague, vacillating, weak willed and sometimes sneaky.

LIBRA DESCENDANT *(ARIES RISING)*

Often criticised as being overtly selfish and too concerned with your own good, you are seeking - whether you know it or not - the more adaptable and compromising type, if only because such a person would complement your energetic individuality. This 'absent' talent for calm compromise you discover in those nice, diplomatic souls with whom you form relationships, and of course, when you venture out into the big wide world, intent on righting wrongs and putting people in their place, you expect total support and attention from your partner. And boy do you lose your patience with them when they refuse to take a firm stand and be positive. All that is happening is that you are drawing from others what is often lacking in yourself, namely the ability to co-operate and be unselfish.

SCORPIO DESCENDANT *(TAURUS RISING)*

Your partner may be a great enigma to you; all this cloak and dagger, intense emotional stuff. Why don't you come out with it and say what is on your mind? Whatever they may be like, you are inwardly seeking a rather forceful and powerful personality in another, someone with a great deal of presence and charisma, and this is precisely what you will attract in the sphere of close relationships. However, there are other items that you will have to put up with: obsessiveness, lack of compromise and emotional complexities, to name only a few out of many, which, believe it or not, are part of your own un-lived psyche.

SAGITTARIUS DESCENDANT *(GEMINI RISING)*

Gemini Rising is seeking to fulfil the 'missing half' through a partner who can bring an overall sense of meaning, some actual point to all of the random facts and figures collected on your journey through life. This Rising Sign often gathers together information for its own sake. In one-to-one relationships it will attract a partner who can offer a more spiritual, philosophical, ultimately deeper meaning to life. On a superficial level, you will attract circumstances through a partner who fulfils your need for freedom, travel, education and a really good laugh, you must have an interesting partner; someone a little different from the rest. A foreigner may suit you, or a person with an unusual past.

CAPRICORN DESCENDANT (CANCER RISING)

In the area of close, personal relationships, you are undoubtedly a cautious, reserved type. This stems from your basic shyness and your inner sense of seriousness about the whole business of one-to-one, give-and-take partnerships. Marriage, for instance, is a particularly serious job, often a heavy responsibility as far as you are concerned, and certainly not something to be treated lightly. In a deep relationship, you discover someone who is likely to be married to you, but also to their work. Within the partnership you continually meet with an emphasis on order. If you are a gregarious and extroverted soul you will find this slightly depressing, even if this disciplined element is just what you need within yourself.

AQUARIUS DESCENDANT (LEO RISING)

With your big-hearted, warm and sunny disposition, and your strong conventional streak, it must come as a surprise for you to discover certain oddball characteristics in those to whom you become close. They often seem so detached, occasionally remote and ultimately concerned with other things: the world out there, society, politics, religion etc. Not all Leo Risings' attract a crazy sociologist, yet there is an element of cool friendliness in the partner as a rule, someone not quite as ego based as your good self; and a person more concerned with the world at large than with the 'me and mine' syndrome. What is more, their opinions are just as strong as yours!

PISCES DESCENDANT (VIRGO RISING)

With your practically-minded, little fuss-pot ways, always being concerned with attention to detail and being effective at your work, it is small wonder that the ambiguous and dreamy elements that you attract in others do not drive you stark staring bonkers. Seriously, within the depths of your psyche, you are seeking a partner who can bring some emotional depth to your world, someone who is open to the flow of life and can offer a glimpse of the rich, feeling universe that you are unconsciously looking for. This would counteract the emphasis you have on duty and attending to the material world. Perhaps you simply desire to escape 'real life' within the sphere of a relationship. The problem is that you have to face up to reality at some stage.

GEMINI IN LOVE

This section is written, not so much with you in mind, but on behalf of those individuals who have already taken the plunge and opted for a life with you, or who may be thinking of doing so. In the appraisal of your birth sign below, and the sections that follow, they may recognise some 'landmarks' that will make the road they walk along with you through life not only more interesting but more rewarding too.

The key to Geminis in emotional relationships is changeability. This means that in their often ambivalent moods Geminis are inclined to treat their partners one day with great love and affection and the next with a remoteness bordering on the chilly.

This is a confusing situation if you happen to be on the receiving end, and unless you are a remarkable person, any changes necessary to accommodate such swings of the pendulum are likely to be made by you! On the other hand, Gemini people are great fun to be with, should be happy more often than they are down and can be guaranteed to bounce back in times of adversity.

The Gemini's first response to love is fairly typical of a person who isn't really in touch with his/her own feelings. The child of Mercury usually goes completely over the top, showering presents galore and a veritable dictionary of fine words upon the object of his/her affection. Alas, with the passing of time a change takes place, Geminis hate routine, so it might be incumbent on you to be as flexible as they are. For your pains you will have gained an interesting and witty pal, who will always keep you entertained and would be willing to talk far into the night, if you can keep up the pace.

Do you want a calm, settled existence, two point five kids and a semi in the suburbs? Perhaps you ought to dip your hand back into the bran-tub of life then, because there is no certainty that you will find any of these forthcoming from a Gemini mate. Of course, you might end up with them all, except for the 'calm' aspect, though I wouldn't count on it. The whole world is home to the Gemini and so travel is a natural part of their lives. On the way they may show you the seven wonders of the world; and living the life that they love, with someone around to help pick up the pieces - they may just prove to be the eighth as far as you are concerned!

GEMINI MEETS GEMINI

This relationship could well be based upon surface attraction, or at a greater depth is apt to be mainly a meeting of minds. How could it be otherwise, when the Gemini temperament is so mentally motivated? Shallowness could be a problem then and it has to be said that there is probably no anchor here sufficient to hold out against the storms of life. It all depends on what you are looking for in the first place, and also on how honest you are willing to be with yourself. True, you will find all the stimulation you could need, and you may not be out to find the bottom of the emotional ocean in any case!

GEMINI MEETS CANCER

A very strange pair of bedfellows these, with a great deal of give and take necessary to bring out the best possibilities of the union. The trouble is that Gemini needs to stretch the net of learning far and wide, whereas Cancer is basically a home-bird and is inclined to crawl back into that crabby shell at the first sign of danger. Whilst Gemini exists on the mental plane of life and is a thinker, the crab has no such lofty pretensions and 'feels'. With each partner's rather different outlook on life, much compromise is needed to make the relationship tick, for while Gemini is inclined to tire of Cancer's introverted, cautious nature, Cancer can become infuriated by the Twins nebulous inconsistency.

GEMINI MEETS LEO

An Air-Fire combination always possesses something rather lively and enthusiastic, and this match is no exception. Here the airy temperament of Gemini keeps the flames of passion alive in Leo. Each is good for the other, as Gemini offers a broader and more intellectual view of life to the often conservative Leo, whilst the Lion assists in bringing a little more warmth and colour into the life of the Gemini. Disagreements could arise as a result of the rather 'rooted' opinions inherent in Leo, which contradict the rapidly changing concepts and opinions of the Twins. Leo is a fixed sign and doesn't like to give ground, whereas Gemini is incapable of losing an argument. There are certain to be sparks here, but then no warming blaze was ever lit without them!

GEMINI MEETS VIRGO

These signs are both ruled by Mercury, which means that communication is the beginning, middle and end of the story. Does this pair ever tire of trying to win the intellectual wrestling match? Probably not. Both partners have sharp analytical minds and good powers of observation. Each considers itself to be quick at verbal retorts and clever puns. Virgo can be incredibly stubborn, though Gemini is mutable enough to cope with this eventuality. In any case, while ever Virgo is stimulated and fulfilled, all should be well. As long as the individuals concerned are happy with a state of constant banter, this looks like a mercurial affair that could well stand the test of time.

GEMINI MEETS LIBRA

Such a sweet pair as this really ought to set an example to others in how to behave in the appropriate manner in a social sense. It is a generally good match for this reason. The typical Gemini has a great liking for the standard Libran, and what better basis is there for starting a personal relationship in the first place? When the pair come together, an air of polite understanding but rapid conversation prevails. Both want to explore life and each knows how to give and accept compliments. Watch out only for too much superficiality and the inability to deal with the mundane tasks of life though, because these two may spend more energy getting out of work than it would take to actually knuckle down and do it.

GEMINI MEETS SCORPIO

Initial magnetism may make this matching appear quite attractive to both parties, for a short while at least. Alas, this could just lead to a terrible mistake. The problem is that Gemini seeks to peer behind the mask that is always worn by the much more secretive Scorpio, whilst Gemini's superficiality eventually proves to be quite unintelligible to the deep, deep Scorpion. Both signs are quite insecure in their own respective ways and each is capable of an air of mystery, albeit displayed in a radically different manner. This is a mutual attraction based on the lure of opposites, which can be a very powerful magnet. When the Scorpio can find lightness of spirit and the Gemini looks hard for his or her own hidden depths, it might just work out.

GEMINI MEETS SAGITTARIUS

Two lively-minded personalities come together here, which although refreshing in many ways, is certain to cause some problems. The potential trouble lies in two such ego-centred natures. It should be remembered that Gemini and Sagittarius are placed opposite each other in the heavens, throwing up the paradox of two personalities that are at first sight very similar, but whose motivations are different. Gemini seeks facts and figures for the sake of doing so, whilst the Archer utilises intuition which allows a view of the picture as a whole. Thus the problem, if one exists, is likely to be one of disagreement over details, because both personalities may come to the same destination, though by different routes.

GEMINI MEETS CAPRICORN

With the strict practicality of Capricorn and the playful changeability of Gemini, it is little wonder that the Goat becomes so aggravated with the Twins at what he or she sees as inconsistency. But the difficulty is more likely to be on the side of the Goat, who is not half so willing to live and let live as Gemini is. Beyond this the match is not a bad one, Gemini helps the Goat to look at life less seriously, whilst the cautious Capricorn can stop the airy Twins from flying too high. Best of all, with the ideas of Gemini and the staying power of Capricorn, business ventures should prosper. Life will rarely be dull!

GEMINI MEETS AQUARIUS

Whilst this pair can, and quite often do, combine very well together, there are certain pitfalls to watch out for. Air signs usually combine successfully, and both Gemini and Aquarius are social animals, enjoying the cut and thrust of stimulating mental interplay. It has to be said however that Aquarians can be a little stubborn, so that whilst adaptability comes as easy as breathing to the Twins, the same is not true of the Water-bearer. Aquarius is a rag-bag of paradoxes, for example loving social groups and yet wanting to be somehow special within them. Gemini, will mix with almost anyone and happily integrate. All in all, communication is the key, and a stimulating relationship can follow, though there must be considerable effort on both sides.

GEMINI MEETS PISCES

There are no degrees about this match, it either works very well
or it doesn't work at all! Pisces is fascinated by the quickfire
humour and verbal dexterity of Gemini and will actively promote
this side of a partner's nature. Meanwhile, adaptable Gemini
looks sympathetically at the far deeper qualities of what is after
all another mutable sign. The fly in the ointment, if there is one,
may come when the child of Mercury begins to tire of plumbing
the seemingly fathomless depths of the Fishes, and the deeper
the probing, the less the response. Once communication breaks
down, difficulties really begin, for what are the Twins without a
wordy interplay? Chatter is a fact of life to the Gemini
individual, so keep the talk coming Mr or Miss Pisces, and don't
sink too deep!

GEMINI MEETS ARIES

Here we are likely to meet a fine, energetic and enthusiastic
meeting of airy and fiery temperaments respectively. The accent
will definitely be on the 'positive' in communication, from both
sides of the divide. There are thrills, spills and much merriment
in store potentially. If the relationship is to be life-long, the test
comes with inevitable change. Working together, and yet as individuals, compromises can be made, with plenty of interests
beyond the relationship and some special give on the part of
Aries where decisions are concerned.

GEMINI MEETS TAURUS

It would be expected that the fascinating charm and chatty manner of the Twins might prove to be particularly attractive when
viewed through the eyes of the more sedate Bull, and indeed this
could see the seeds of a relationship between the two being sown.
Perhaps the signs are too close together in space though, for
there is little that the Bull can offer to Gemini that it doesn't already possess in abundance; be it charm, wit, gregariousness or
a love of life. Gemini may well find Taurus to be a little dull on
occasions, whilst the poor Bull is wound up to the point of utter
frustration in trying to follow the intricate flight of the zodiac's
butterfly. Both signs have the ability to eat away at potential
problems, but would they really want to try? The answer could
be no, but stranger matches have worked remarkably well.

THE MOON AND YOUR DAY TO DAY LIFE

Look up at the sky on most cloudless nights and you are almost certain to see the Earth's closest neighbour in space, engaged in her frighteningly complicated relationship with the planet on which we live. The Moon isn't very large, in fact only a small fraction of the size of our own planet, but it is very close to us in spacial terms and herein lies the reason for the Moon having a greater part to play in our day to day lives than almost any other body in space.

People have realised for centuries that ocean tides are regulated by the Moon, but it doesn't stop there. Practically all life responds to the subtle gravitational and magnetic forces created when the Moon is closest to our planet or when she passes overhead. We, human beings, merely another form of life, are not immune to the same cyclic forces that have helped to shape the face of this our spaceship home.

The very brain that allows us to think and act in the way that we do is composed of 90% water. Since the Moon can generate tides in a body of liquid as small as that contained in a teacup, it isn't surprising to learn that the whole of our watery mass, and particularly that saturated brain, is also subjected to tidal forces. It is fair to say, in astrological terms, that if the Sun and planets represent the hour and minute hands regulating our character swings and mood changes, the Moon is the rapidly sweeping second hand, governing emotions especially, but touching practically every aspect of human life.

The reason that 'popular' astrology doesn't deal more specifically with the part that our closest neighbour in space plays in our daily lives is mainly because the Moon moves so quickly and maintains a staggeringly complex orbital relationship with the Earth. However, since no book professing to chart the ups and downs of your daily life could possible be complete without some reference to lunar fluctuations, I have worked hard to include, not one, but two separate ways through which you can recognise and understand how you slot into some of the lunar cycles, and then go on to learn why this knowledge is so important. The first of these deals with the fascinating relationship between the Earth's lanterns by night and day, and the way that they relate to each other.

SUN MOON CYCLES

The first lunar cycle dealt with in Old Moore's Horoscope and Astral Diary concerns the relationship between the Moon and and your own personal zodiac Sun-sign. We have made the fluctuations of this pattern easy for you to understand by means of a simple cyclic graph. It appears on the first page of each 'Your Month At A Glance'. under the title of 'Highs and Lows'. Each graph displays the lunar cycle for the month to come and you will soon learn how its movements have a bearing on your energy and abilities. Once you recognise the patterns, you can work within them, making certain that your maximum efforts are expended at the most opportune time.

MOON AGE CYCLES

The second method of referring to the lunar patterns that help to make you feel the way that you do on any particular day is a little more complicated and involves a small amount of work on your part to establish where you slot into the rhythms. However, since Moon Age Cycles are one of the most potent astrological forces at work in your life, the effort is more than worthwhile.

The Moon Age Cycle refers to the way that the date of your birth fits into the Moon's Phase patterns. Because of the complex relationship of the Earth and the Moon, we can see the face of the lunar disc apparently changing throughout a period of roughly one month. In fact the word month comes from the same root source as the word moon itself. The period between one New Moon (the time at which the Moon is invisible from the Earth) and the next is about 29 days. Between the two an observer would have seen more and more of the Moon's face on successive nights until Full Moon, after which the face of the Moon grows smaller and smaller for the remainder of the period. We call this cycle the Moon Age Cycle and classify the day of the New Moon as day 0. Full Moon occurs on day 15, with the next New Moon returning on day 28 or 29. dependent on the complicated motions of the combined Earth and Moon.

If you know in which Moon Age Day you were born, then you also know how you fit into the cycle. You would monitor the changes of the cycle as more or less tension in your body, an easy or strained disposition, good or bad temper and so on. What you have to do to ascertain your Moon Age Day is to look at the two

New Moon Tables on pages 33 and 34. Down the left-hand column you will see every year between 1900 and 1992 listed, and the months of the year appear across the top. Where the year of your birth and the month in which you were born coincide, the figure shown indicates the day of the month on which New Moon occurred. You need to pick the New Moon immediately prior to your birth, so if your birthday falls at or near to the beginning of a month, it might be necessary to refer to the New Moon in the previous month. Once you have established the New Moon immediately prior to your day of birth (and of course in the correct year) all you have to do is to count forward to your birthday.

Don't forget that the day of the New Moon is classed as 0. As an example, if you were born on March 22nd 1962, the last New Moon prior to your date of birth occurred on March 6th 1962. Counting forward from the 6th to the 22nd would mean that the day of your birth happened on Moon Age Day 16. If your Moon Age Cycle crosses the end of February, don't forget to check that you were not born in a leap year.

HOW TO USE MOON AGE DAYS

Once you have established your personal Moon Age Day, you can refer to the Diary section of the book because there, listed next to each day, is the Moon Sign and also the Moon Age Day. The Moon Age Day in each month that coincides with your own should find you on a noticeable intellectual and physical high. At such times you will feel generally more settled and your thinking processes should be clear and concise. There are other important days in the cycle that you will want to look at too, and to make matters easier I have compiled an easy to follow chart on pages 35 and 36. Quite soon you will come to understand which Moon Age Days influence you, and how.

Don't forget that Moon Age cycles, although specific to your date of birth, also run within other important astrological patterns that you will also find described in this book. So, for example, if your Moon Age Day looked good on a particular day of the month, but everything else was working to the contrary, you might be wise to delay any particularly monumental effort until another more generally favourable day. Sometimes cycles run together and often they do not, which is part of the reason why you periodically feel that you could run the world single-handed and yet at other times you cannot seem to do anything right.

HOW TO USE THE MOON AGE QUICK REFERENCE TABLE (PAGES 35&36)

The most important factor that you can discover about yourself in terms of Moon Age cycles, is the way that your emotions are holding up day by day. Your emotional stability, or lack of it, inevitably spills over into every other sphere of your daily behaviour and therefore contributes to your successes or failures. Knowing in advance on which days you are likely to be at your most dynamic can be of great assistance in planning your schedules. It also follows that on days indicated as being less emotionally assertive, you can take life a little more steadily and even gently forgive yourself for your human fallibility. It isn't an excuse for refusing to try, simply a way of learning the best times for the greatest efforts.

Across the top of the table locate your own personal Moon Age Day. Now follow the column down vertically. Here you will find a list of + and - symbols, together with one * symbol. By tracing across to the left, you can see at which days in the Moon Age Cycle the symbols appear. Now that you know when your assertive and passive days occur on the Moon Age Quick Reference Table, you can, if you wish, place them in the appropriate days in the Diary, so that you will always know in advance what the Moon Age Cycle is doing for you personally. The + symbol indicates days when you are feeling more emotionally 'in tune' and secure. Decisions made on such days are liable to be based on a sounder reasoning principle and usually will not have to be thought out again later. You may also notice that you are more friendly, caring and sharing.

The - symbol should not be considered as entirely negative. It merely indicates that on these days you are probably quieter, more contemplative and not especially assertive. We all have periods when meditation would do us more good than phrenetic activity and the - days could well be such times for you.

Look carefully for the * symbol, because this represents your Moon Age Birthday for each month, (in fact you will occasionally have two in a calendar month). As long as other cycles agree, this should be an especially good day for making the sort of long-term decisions that require deep insight and faith in your own abilities.

Days which carry no symbol at all indicate an emotionally neutral period, at which time you will be responding predominantly to other astrological cycles.

NEW MOON TABLE

YEAR	JAN	FEB	MAR	APR	MAY	JUN	JUL	AUG	SEP	OCT	NOV	DEC
1901	21	19	20	19	18	16	15	14	12	10	10	10
1902	9	8	9	8	7	6	5	3	2	1/30	29	29
1903	27	26	28	27	26	25	24	22	21	20	19	18
1904	17	15	17	16	15	14	14	12	10	18	8	8
1905	6	5	5	4	3	2	2/31	30	28	28	26	26
1906	24	23	24	23	22	21	20	19	18	17	16	15
1907	14	12	14	12	11	10	9	8	7	6	5	5
1908	3	2	3	2	1/30	29	28	27	25	25	24	24
1909	22	20	21	20	19	17	17	15	14	14	13	12
1910	11	9	11	9	9	7	6	5	3	2	1	1/30
1911	29	28	30	28	28	26	25	24	22	21	20	20
1912	18	17	19	18	17	16	15	13	12	11	9	9
1913	7	6	7	6	5	4	3	2/31	30	29	28	27
1914	25	24	26	24	24	23	22	21	19	19	17	17
1915	15	14	15	13	13	12	11	10	9	8	7	6
1916	5	3	5	3	2	1/30	30	29	27	27	26	25
1917	24	22	23	22	20	19	18	17	15	15	14	13
1918	12	11	12	11	10	8	8	6	4	4	3	2
1919	1/31	-	2/31	30	29	27	27	25	23	23	22	21
1920	21	19	20	18	18	16	15	14	12	12	10	10
1921	9	8	9	8	7	6	5	3	2	1/30	29	29
1922	27	26	28	27	26	25	24	22	21	20	19	18
1923	17	15	17	16	15	14	14	12	10	10	8	8
1924	6	5	5	4	3	2	2/31	30	28	28	26	26
1925	24	23	24	23	22	21	20	19	18	17	16	15
1926	14	12	14	12	11	10	9	8	7	6	5	5
1927	3	2	3	2	1/30	29	28	27	25	25	24	24
1928	21	19	21	20	19	18	17	16	14	14	12	12
1929	11	9	11	9	9	7	6	5	3	2	1	1/30
1930	29	28	30	28	28	26	25	24	22	20	20	19
1931	18	17	19	18	17	16	15	13	12	11	9	9
1932	7	6	7	6	5	4	3	2/31	30	29	2	27
1933	25	24	26	24	24	23	22	21	19	19	17	17
1934	15	14	15	13	13	12	11	10	9	8	7	6
1935	5	3	5	3	2	1/30	30	29	27	27	26	25
1936	24	22	23	21	20	19	18	17	15	15	14	13
1937	12	11	12	12	10	8	8	6	4	4	3	2
1938	1/31	-	2/31	30	29	27	27	25	23	23	22	21
1939	20	19	20	19	19	17	16	15	13	12	11	10
1940	9	8	9	7	7	6	5	4	2	1/30	29	28
1941	27	26	27	26	26	24	24	22	21	20	19	18
1942	16	15	16	15	15	13	13	12	10	10	8	8
1943	6	4	6	4	4	2	2	1/30	29	29	27	27
1944	25	24	24	22	22	20	20	18	17	17	15	15
1945	14	12	14	12	11	10	9	8	6	6	4	4
1946	3	2	3	2	1/30	29	28	26	25	24	23	23

NEW MOON TABLE

YEAR	JAN	FEB	MAR	APR	MAY	JUN	JUL	AUG	SEP	OCT	NOV	DEC
1947	21	19	21	20	19	18	17	16	14	14	12	12
1948	11	9	11	9	9	7	6	5	3	2	1	1/30
1949	29	27	29	28	27	26	25	24	23	21	20	19
1950	18	16	18	17	17	15	15	13	12	11	9	9
1951	7	6	7	6	6	4	4	2	1	1/30	29	28
1952	26	25	25	24	23	22	23	20	29	28	27	27
1953	15	14	15	13	13	11	11	9	8	8	6	6
1954	5	3	5	3	2	1/30	29	28	27	26	25	25
1955	24	22	24	22	21	20	19	17	16	15	14	14
1956	13	11	12	11	10	8	8	6	4	4	2	2
1957	1/30	-	1/31	29	29	27	27	25	23	23	21	21
1958	19	18	20	19	18	17	16	15	13	12	11	10
1959	9	7	9	8	7	6	6	4	3	2/31	30	29
1960	27	26	27	26	26	24	24	22	21	20	19	18
1961	16	15	16	15	14	13	12	11	10	9	8	7
1962	6	5	6	5	4	2	1/31	30	28	28	27	26
1963	25	23	25	23	23	21	20	19	17	17	15	15
1964	14	13	14	12	11	10	9	7	6	5	4	4
1965	3	1	2	1	1/30	29	28	26	25	24	22	22
1966	21	19	21	20	19	18	17	16	14	14	12	12
1967	10	9	10	9	8	7	7	5	4	3	2	1/30
1968	29	28	29	28	27	26	25	24	23	22	21	20
1969	1 9	17	18	16	15	14	13	12	11	10	9	9
1970	7	6	7	6	6	4	4	2	1	1/30	29	28
1971	26	25	26	25	24	22	22	20	19	19	18	17
1972	15	14	15	13	13	11	11	9	8	8	6	6
1973	5	4	5	3	2	1/30	29	28	27	26	25	25
1974	24	22	24	22	21	20	19	17	16	15	14	14
1975	12	11	12	11	11	9	9	7	5	5	3	3
1976	1/31	29	30	29	29	27	27	25	23	23	21	21
1977	19	18	19	18	18	16	16	14	13	12	11	10
1978	9	7	9	7	7	5	5	4	2	2/31	30	29
1979	27	26	27	26	26	24	24	22	21	20	19	18
1980	16	15	16	15	14	13	12	11	10	9	8	7
1981	6	4	6	4	4	2	1/31	29	28	27	26	26
1982	25	23	24	23	21	21	20	19	17	17	15	15
1983	14	13	14	13	12	11	10	8	7	6	4	4
1984	3	1	2	1	1/30	29	28	26	25	24	22	22
1985	21	19	21	20	19	18	17	16	14	14	12	12
1986	10	9	10	9	8	7	7	5	4	3	2	1/30
1987	29	28	29	28	27	26	25	24	23	22	21	20
1988	19	17	18	16	15	14	13	12	11	10	9	9
1989	7	6	7	6	5	3	3	1/31	29	29	28	28
1990	26	25	26	25	24	22	22	20	19	18	17	17
1991	15	14	15	13	13	11	11	9	8	8	6	6
1992	4	3	4	3	2	1/30	29	28	26	25	24	24

MOON AGE QUICK REFERENCE TABLE

YOUR OWN MOON AGE DAY

MOON AGE CALENDAR	1	2	3	4	5	6	7	8	9	10	11	12	13	14	15
0				+		+			-			+		+	
1	*				+	+	+		-				+		+
2		*				+		+			-			+	+
3			*				+		+		-				+
4		+		*				+		+			-		
5			+		*				+		+			-	
6	+			+		*				+		+			-
7		+			+		*				+		+		
8	-		+			+		*				+		+	
9		-		+			+		*				+		+
10	+		-		+			+		*				+	+
11		+		-		+			+		*				+
12	+		+		-		+			+		*			
13		+		+		-		+			+		*		
14			+		+		-		+			+		*	
15	-			+		+			-		+		+		*
16		-			+		+		-		+			+	
17	+		-			+		+	-			+			+
19		+		-			+		+	-			+		
19	+		+		-			+		+		-		+	+
20		+		+		-			+		+		-		+
21			+		+		-			+		+		-	
22	-			+		+		-			+		+	+	-
23		-			+		+	-				+		+	
24			-			+		+		-			+	+	
25	+			-			+		+		-			+	
26		+			-			+		+		-			+
27	+		+			-			+		+		-		
28		+		+			-			+		+		-	
29			+		+			-				+		+	-

35

MOON AGE QUICK REFERENCE TABLE

YOUR OWN MOON AGE DAY

	16	17	18	19	20	21	22	23	24	25	26	27	28	29	0
0	-			+		+		-		+			+		*
1		-			+		+		-		+			+	
2	+		-			+		+		-		+			+
3		+		-			+		+		-		+		
4	+		+		-			+		+		-		+	
5		+		+		-			+		+		-		+
6			+		+		-			+		+		-	
7	-			+		+		-			+		+		-
8		-			+		+		-			+		+	
9			-			+		+		-			+		+
10	+			-			+		+		-			+	
11		+			-			+		+		-			+
12	+		+			-			+		+		-		
13		+		+			-			+		+		-	
14			+		+			-			+		+		-
15				+		+			-			+		+	
16	*			+		+			-			+		+	
17		*				+		+			-			+	
18	+		*				+		+			-			+
19		+		*				+		+			-		
20			+		*				+		+			-	
21	+			+		*				+		+			-
22		+			+		*				+		+		
23	-		+			+		*				+		+	
24		-		+			+		*				+		+
25	+		-		+			+		*				+	
26		+		-		+			+		*				+
27	+		+		-		+			+		*			
28		+		+		-		+			+		*		
29			+		+		-		+			+		*	

The vertical label on the left reads: MOON AGE CALENDAR

36

THE ASTRAL DIARY

How the diagrams work

Each month I have produced a set of simple *picture diagrams* to show you when and where the influences may be pushing and pulling. I believe that from these *diagrams* you get the most personal information that you can buy anywhere.

Through these *picture diagrams* I want to help you to plot your year. With them you can see where the positive and negative aspects will be found each month. To make the most of them all you have to do is remember where and when!

Let me show you how they work . . .

THE MONTH AT A GLANCE

Just as there are twelve separate Zodiac Signs, so Astrologers believe that each sign has twelve separate aspects to life. For instance, ONE represents the strength of your Personality: TWO Your Personal Finance: FIVE Pleasure and Romance: TEN Your Career Aspirations. Each of the Twelve segments relates to a different personal aspect. I number and list them all every month as a key so that you don't have to remember them all for yourself.

The twelve major aspects of your life

Shading inside the box means 'ordinary'

Symbols above the box means 'positive'

1	2	3	4	5	6	7	8	9	10	11	12

Symbol below the box means 'negative'

I have designed this chart to show you how and when these twelve different aspects are being influenced throughout the year. Where a number rests comfortably in its shaded box, nothing out of the ordinary is to be expected. However, when a box turns white then you should expect influences to become active in this area of your life. Where the influence is positive, I have raised a smiling sun above its number. Where it is a negative, I hang a little rain cloud beneath it.

By noting which aspects of your life are going to be influenced throughout the year, and how, you can build yourself a picture of when and where your opportunities may be and where or when you may need to make a greater effort to overcome a difficult influence.

YOUR ENERGY-RHYTHM CHART

In this *picture diagram* I am linking your Zodiac Group to the rhythm of the moon. In doing this I have calculated when you will be gaining strength from its influence and equally when you may be weakened by it.

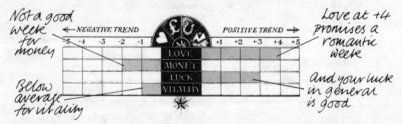

At your best on 11th – 12th

Gradually falling energy from 12th – 25th

Increasing energy as the month starts

Things are picking up

Take it easy on the 24th!

If you think of yourself as being like the tides of the ocean then you may understand how your own energies must rise and fall too. And if you understand how it works and when it is working, then you can better organise your activities to achieve more and get things done more easily.

MOVING-PICTURE-SCREEN
measured every week
LOVE, LUCK, MONEY & VITALITY

Not a good week for money

Below average for vitality

Love at +4 promises a romantic week

And your luck in general is good

I hope that this offers more than a little bit of fun. It is very easy to use. The Bars move across the scale to give you some idea of the strength of opportunities open to you in each of the four areas. If LOVE stands at plus 4, then get out and put yourself about, because in terms of Romance, things should be going your way. When the Bar moves backwards then the opportunities are weakening and when it enters the Negative Scale, then Romance shouldn't be at the top of your list, should it?

Have fun with my *picture diagrams* and keep using them to remind yourself where you are now — and where you are going to be!

Happy New Year

OCTOBER
1992

YOUR MONTH AT A GLANCE

The twelve numbered boxes represent the important areas in your life. The key to the numbers you will find beneath the panel. A Sun above the number indicates that opportunities are around. A Cloud below the number, that you should be a bit defensive. Nothing above or below and life will be pretty ordinary.

1	☀2	3	☀4	5	6	☀7	8	9	10	11	12
	☁			☁			☁				

KEY

1 Strength of Personality
2 Personal Finance
3 Useful Information Gathering
4 Domestic Affairs
5 Pleasure & Romance
6 Effective Work & Health

7 One to One Relationships
8 Questioning, Thinking & Deciding
9 External Influences / Education
10 Career Aspirations
11 Teamwork Activities
12 Unconscious Impulses

OCTOBER HIGHS AND LOWS

Here, I show how the rhythm of the Moon will affect you this month. Like the tide, your energies and abilities will rise and fall with its pattern. When it is above the date line, go-for-it. When it is below the line you should be resting.

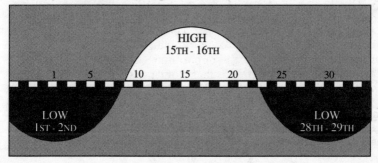

HIGH
15TH - 16TH

1   5   10   15   20   25   30

LOW
1ST - 2ND

LOW
28TH - 29TH

5 MONDAY
Moon Phase Day 9 • Moon Sign Aquarius

am ....

pm ....

The fact that Venus is presently in your sixth house contributes to a general feeling of laziness that rests around you at present. The only way to shift this lethargy is to make certain that the things you are doing captivate all your imagination and not simply a part of it. Friends can cause concern.

6 TUESDAY
Moon Phase Day 10 • Moon Sign Aquarius

am ....

pm ....

Tasks are still likely to go unfinished and this may be partly due to the fact that Jupiter now passes into your solar fifth house, increasing popularity and diverting your mind away from some of the practicalities of life. This would not be a fortunate period for judging the behaviour of others at all!

7 WEDNESDAY
Moon Phase Day 11 • Moon Sign Aquarius

am ....

pm ....

For once you can watch and wait, something that you are not exactly famous for as a rule. Things that you don't have time to get done are certain to wait for a day or two, though you should be more effective in your ability to sort out the lives of people who are dear to you. Keep a tight hold on your cash resources.

8 THURSDAY
Moon Phase Day 12 • Moon Sign Pisces

am ....

pm ....

With help surrounding you at work, the practicalities of life take on a more useful aspect and you find that you are able to get masses more done than you probably expected. The countdown to an important social event starts now and some careful planning is necessary as a result. The attitudes of family members are variable.

9 FRIDAY
Moon Phase Day 13 • Moon Sign Pisces

am ....

pm ....

Because you are presently good mannered and helpful in the ex-treme, you should not be too surprised at the level of assistance that is coming back at you from other directions. Rules and regulations may get on your nerves and there is great reason to be patient with authority figures, who may have your interests at heart.

10 SATURDAY
Moon Phase Day 14 • Moon Sign Aries

am ....

pm ....

Now that Jupiter is firmly in your solar fifth house there is definite-ly an air of financial optimism about and so you have good reason to believe that you can afford to spoil yourself a little. Romance also figures in your life, particularly in terms of the attention that you are receiving from your partner.

11 SUNDAY
Moon Phase Day 15 • Moon Sign Aries

am ....

pm ....

A time of balance and equilibrium in all things is evident, so much so that many situations should resolve themselves, almost without any intervention on your part. No matter how much you feel you have to do at home, Sunday should mean time to relax and the people that you care about the most are willing to agree.

← NEGATIVE TREND   POSITIVE TREND →

	-5	-4	-3	-2	-1		+1	+2	+3	+4	+5
LOVE							▓	▓			
MONEY		▓	▓	▓	▓						
LUCK							▓				
VITALITY				▓	▓						

41

12 MONDAY
Moon Phase Day 16 • Moon Sign Aries

am ....

pm ....

Energy is on the increase, so don't be surprised if the start of the working week finds you getting through much more work than you may have expected. There is always time to spare to consider matters that lie outside your workaday life however and you desperately need the relaxation that can attend friendships.

13 TUESDAY
Moon Phase Day 17 • Moon Sign Taurus

am ....

pm ....

Although today should be just as easy-going as yesterday, it has the additional advantage of being more practical in terms of the decisions that you make and the many ideas that you have for the future. Conversations come thick and fast from all directions, and some of them could easily start you thinking differently.

14 WEDNESDAY
Moon Phase Day 18 • Moon Sign Taurus

am ....

pm ....

There is a winning streak on the way, mainly funded by the sort of innovative ideas that you are so famous for. Although you would not be advised to involve yourself in financial gambles just at present, chances that you are willing to take in other directions do show a tendency to work out to your advantage.

15 THURSDAY
Moon Phase Day 19 • Moon Sign Gemini

am ....

pm ....

Here comes your lunar high, the period when the Moon occupies your Sun-sign. At such times your energy level is especially high and most of the projects that have been waiting in the wings show a tendency to be working out to your advantage. The only thing that you have to avoid is trying to take on too much.

16 FRIDAY   *Moon Phase Day 20 • Moon Sign Gemini*

am ....

pm ....

A day to be thinking about career prospects and what you can do to improve them somewhat. You can be quite calculating just now, a fact that is not lost on many of the people that you come across in your daily life. Most of them should be more than willing to help you out as much as they can in the days ahead.

17 SATURDAY   *Moon Phase Day 21• Moon Sign Cancer*

am ....

pm ....

Although you may well be taking liberties with finances, you do have the cheek to pull off a major personal coup, though it could be a close run thing and it isn't wise to put more pressure on yourself at present than you know is reasonable or good for you.   Others will consider that your behaviour is rash.

18 SUNDAY   *Moon Phase Day 22 • Moon Sign Cancer*

am ....

pm ....

Problems at home, especially those related to the attitudes and feelings of close relatives, need to be dealt with as quickly as possible if you are going to get the most out of this Sunday. There is little chance to rest on your laurels or to smart-talk your way through any situation. Confidence isn't so high.

← *NEGATIVE TREND*   *POSITIVE TREND* →

-5	-4	-3	-2	-1		+1	+2	+3	+4	+5
					LOVE					
					MONEY					
					LUCK					
					VITALITY					

19 MONDAY

Moon Phase Day 23 • Moon Sign Leo

am ....

pm ....

Close relationships improve, perhaps just in time for you to get back to work. What you view at the moment is a world that isn't entirely working to your advantage, and the feeling that perhaps you got out of bed on the wrong side. Look for life's natural advantages and use them to colour the greys of your own day.

20 TUESDAY

Moon Phase Day 24 • Moon Sign Leo

am ....

pm ....

In both business and pleasure you are now able to come to terms with the people that life is throwing into your path. Gemini powers of communication are rarely diminished for very long and many of the advantages that appear down to fate are in reality at least partly thanks to the silver tongue that occupies your head.

21 WEDNESDAY

Moon Phase Day 25 • Moon Sign Leo

am ....

pm ....

The present position of Venus is apt to indicate a closer alliance with someone who has not figured so strongly in your life in the past. This would be the case particularly for younger or unattached Geminis because the planet of love inevitably points in the direction of romance. Keep an eye on wayward relatives.

22 THURSDAY

Moon Phase Day 26 • Moon Sign Virgo

am ....

pm ....

In a domestic sense at least, life should be running very smoothly. There is a possibility that irritations could attend your working life, if so the best course of action would be to talk things through in an attempt to convince colleagues that your point of view is both sensible and practical.

23 FRIDAY
Moon Phase Day 27 • Moon Sign Virgo

am ....

pm ....

Organisation skills are evident as the Sun enters your solar sixth house. You can look forward to a period over the next month or so when all that you hold dearest to your heart becomes a distinct possibility. Casual conversations throw up some surprising facts and cause a lateral shift in your thinking.

24 SATURDAY
Moon Phase Day 28 • Moon Sign Libra

am ....

pm ....

Because you are feeling in a particularly dutiful frame of mind you will be anxious to turn your many skills towards improving the lot of the people who are dear to you, and also looking at the problems of a greater world beyond your own door. Capitalise on recent situations at home that are coming good.

25 SUNDAY
Moon Phase Day 0 • Moon Sign Libra

am ....

pm..

What could well be a time of celebration for the folk you live with can be less than interesting to you, and as a result you are far more likely to be turning your attention towards the needs and wants of friends. Minor frustrations early in the day should not be allowed to distract you from pursuing important objectives.

← NEGATIVE TREND							POSITIVE TREND →			
-5	-4	-3	-2	-1		+1	+2	+3	+4	+5
					LOVE					
					MONEY					
					LUCK					
					VITALITY					

26 MONDAY
Moon Phase Day 1 • Moon Sign Scorpio

am ....

pm ....

Work drops into the background and you opt instead for giving some more thought to the way that your social life is developing. Critics abound, especially in matters that you may have asked for assistance with previously, though it is now important to make it plain that you know what you are doing and should be left alone to do it.

27 TUESDAY
Moon Phase Day 2 • Moon Sign Scorpio

am ....

pm ....

Keep an eye out for invitations that once again turn your life in the direction of social possibilities. Work can be a drag and there is a definite restlessness around just at present that demands your attention. As a result it wouldn't be a bad idea to ring the changes and spend a few hours doing something different.

28 WEDNESDAY
Moon Phase Day 3 • Moon Sign Sagittarius

am ....

pm ....

With the lunar low entering your life for the second time in a month, you stand a chance of finishing the month at a low ebb, that is unless you accept the limitations about you and find ways to turn them to your advantage. Keep up a hectic pace at your peril, when you could be comfortable planning and getting some rest!

29 THURSDAY
Moon Phase Day 4 • Moon Sign Sagittarius

am ....

pm ....

Confidence isn't high, though there are people about who should be more than willing to offer you a boost. While you are feeling that you are knocking your head against a brick wall, especially in a personal sense, the batteries of your life are re-charging themselves and everything is working out as it should.

30 FRIDAY

Moon Phase Day 5 • Moon Sign Capricorn

am ....

pm ....

Better times are in the offing. Now that the Moon has left your opposite sign, things slowly start to improve, starting with your personal life, in which your nearest and dearest appear to have a better understanding of the things that you are trying to say to them. Confidence is also higher at work.

31 SATURDAY

Moon Phase Day 6 • Moon Sign Capricorn

am ....

pm ....

A generally good end to the month. There are new possibilities beginning to show themselves on the home front and relationships should be working out quite well. Creature comforts become more important and there could be more money around than has been the case for a short while, though it's important to spend wisely.

1 SUNDAY

Moon Phase Day 7 • Moon Sign Capricorn

am ....

pm ....

You are a real busy beaver as the month of November commences, anxious to get the most out of life and eager to do what you can to improve the lot of your nearest and dearest. As usual you have plenty to say for yourself and shouldn't go short of people who are captivated by your mercurial charm and so are listening.

NEGATIVE TREND								POSITIVE TREND			
-5	-4	-3	-2	-1			+1	+2	+3	+4	+5
					LOVE						
					MONEY						
					LUCK						
					VITALITY						

NOVEMBER
1992
YOUR MONTH AT A GLANCE

The twelve numbered boxes represent the important areas in your life. The key to the numbers you will find beneath the panel. A Sun above the number indicates that opportunities are around. A Cloud below the number, that you should be a bit defensive. Nothing above or below and life will be pretty ordinary.

1	2	3	4	5	6	7	8	9	10	11	12

KEY

1 Strength of Personality
2 Personal Finance
3 Useful Information Gathering
4 Domestic Affairs
5 Pleasure & Romance
6 Effective Work & Health

7 One to One Relationships
8 Questioning, Thinking & Deciding
9 External Influences / Education
10 Career Aspirations
11 Teamwork Activities
12 Unconscious Impulses

NOVEMBER HIGHS AND LOWS

Here, I show how the rhythm of the Moon will affect you this month. Like the tide, your energies and abilities will rise and fall with its pattern. When it is above the date line, go-for-it. When it is below the line you should be resting.

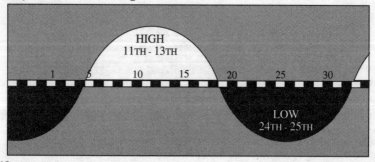

HIGH
11TH - 13TH

LOW
24TH - 25TH

48

2 MONDAY

Moon Phase Day 8 • Moon Sign Aquarius

am ....

pm ....

A sense of happy contentedness permeates your personal life, even if you don't actually register the fact as the day opens. At least this means that you have more energy to get on with the routines of life and even to enjoy them for a change. Venus is strong in your seventh house, so watch out for romantic prospects.

3 TUESDAY

Moon Phase Day 9 • Moon Sign Aquarius

am ....

pm ....

With an urge to spread your wings at the moment, there appears to be very little that would keep you in one place for very long. Attention to detail is now much harder to find and so there is a possibility that some important tasks will remain unfinished. Changes are important, but so are practicalities.

4 WEDNESDAY

Moon Phase Day 10 • Moon Sign Pisces

am ....

pm ....

Energy is still with you, so do almost anything that takes your fancy. With a high level of popularity you are inclined to be basking in the attention that comes your way from a host of different directions. The general need now is for balance, something that you don't have in great abundance.

5 THURSDAY

Moon Phase Day 11• Moon Sign Pisces

am ....

pm ....

Effort is dissipated in every conceivable direction, so be careful today that you don't subject yourself to minor mishaps and accidents simply because you are not taking enough notice of what is going on around you. However, even when you think you must be flagging, more energy comes along.

6 FRIDAY

Moon Phase Day 12 • Moon Sign Pisces

am ....

pm ....

Anyone other than a Gemini would take some time today to sit back and appreciate all that they had achieved during the last few days. Not so in your case, though you would be well advised to recognise the signs that say 'enough is enough'. Your capacity for life knows no bounds but you are only human!

7 SATURDAY

Moon Phase Day 13 • Moon Sign Aries

am ....

pm ....

Pay some attention to relationships, especially at a personal level. Overspending may have been a problem and if so there may be nothing for it but to sit down with a pen and paper and work things out. If things are really out of hand, there should be someone around who would be willing to lend a hand.

8 SUNDAY

Moon Phase Day 14 • Moon Sign Aries

am ....

pm ....

It is partly because you are in such a generous mood that things may have gone a little haywire in the fiscal sector of your life. Still nothing puts a curb on your kindness, even when others should be spending money on you. Just ensure that you are not being taken advantage of and that you have your wits about you.

← *NEGATIVE TREND*   *POSITIVE TREND* →

-5	-4	-3	-2	-1		+1	+2	+3	+4	+5
					LOVE					
					MONEY					
					LUCK					
					VITALITY					

9 MONDAY
Moon Phase Day 15 • Moon Sign Taurus

am ....

pm ....

It is an odds on certainty that you are at last looking more carefully at the money that you have and the way it is being spent. Turn a little mean for once, though as always you need to avoid pendulum swings and would be much better off looking for a middle path to follow. Friends can be quite irksome.

10 TUESDAY
Moon Phase Day 16 • Moon Sign Taurus

am ....

pm ....

Because an unusual but very welcome patient streak begins to exhibit itself today, you can get a host of little jobs out of the way and end up feeling that at last you are beginning to make the sort of practical progress that is so important to you. Don't hold your breath though, times change quickly in your life.

11 WEDNESDAY
Moon Phase Day 17 • Moon Sign Gemini

am ....

pm ....

The lunar high arrives and puts all the pep into your life again. Mid-week misunderstandings can soon be cleared up and you show a profound intuition when it comes to understanding what makes people behave in the way that they do. Whilst other folk choose to creep about quietly, you display your customary exuberance.

12 THURSDAY
Moon Phase Day 18 • Moon Sign Gemini

am ....

pm ....

Today you can approach some very influential people in the certain knowledge that at least your ideas will be listened to carefully and that you have the advantage of a charming disposition when it comes to putting your point of view. New projects commenced at this time have a good chance of succeeding.

13 FRIDAY
Moon Phase Day 19 • Moon Sign Gemini

am ....

pm ....

Your partner or a close friend begins to have a more profound part to play in both your thinking processes and in the way that situations are inclined to turn out generally. Putting on a good show is what you are all about, so if there is any presentation in the offing, you can be relied upon to make it buzz.

14 SATURDAY
Moon Phase Day 20 • Moon Sign Cancer

am ....

pm ....

The spirit of co-operation is alive and well inside your noble and magnanimous chest today. This is a wonderful time astrologically to enjoy a family motivated weekend, and also to leave some time for friends who may have been pushed slightly into the background of late. Old dilemmas fade away now.

15 SUNDAY
Moon Phase Day 21 • Moon Sign Cancer

am ....

pm ....

Have you ever been accused of being enigmatic? Whether you have or not in the past, prepare yourself for the experience now. The thing is that you say a great deal and yet in some ways you say very little, especially about your own soul and what motivates you to take the sort of actions that you do.

NEGATIVE TREND						POSITIVE TREND				
-5	-4	-3	-2	-1		+1	+2	+3	+4	+5
					LOVE					
					MONEY					
					LUCK					
					VITALITY					

16 MONDAY

Moon Phase Day 22 • Moon Sign Leo

am ....

pm ....

All matters should be mulled over carefully and no decision taken until you are certain that you have heard every point of view fully. It is patently obvious that not everyone you come across can be telling you the truth, but there are some convincing liars about, even if they only really deceive themselves.

17 TUESDAY

Moon Phase Day 23 • Moon Sign Leo

am ....

pm ....

If you were expecting life to hand out justice all around today, you had better think again. Of course, as the scales of karma tip gently one way and then another, the balance is ultimately achieved, but it won't look that way at all for now. Listen, watch and wait to see what comes along in the way of advice.

18 WEDNESDAY

Moon Phase Day 24 • Moon Sign Virgo

am ....

pm ....

Today is apt to be very slow, not at all what you have come to expect over the last couple of weeks. It isn't that things are going wrong exactly, more that there are delays and hold-ups that have a tendency to get on your nerves. Better times follow on and for the moment you could do worse than to relax.

19 THURSDAY

Moon Phase Day 25 • Moon Sign Virgo

am ....

pm ....

Tackling problems head on is the only way that you know how to behave, though this might not be the technique that other people want to adopt. Remember the adage 'softly, softly, catchee monkey' because it is really appropriate to some of the situations that permeate your life at the present time.

20 FRIDAY
Moon Phase Day 26 • Moon Sign Libra

am ....

pm ....

You carry so much natural wisdom around in your head that you are sometimes inclined to forget that you have learned so much. This is a strange day because it appears that the good advice you are so willing to dish out to other people is equally appropriate to your own life, yet you fail to recognise the fact.

21 SATURDAY
Moon Phase Day 27 • Moon Sign Libra

am ....

pm ....

Attached Geminis should find support coming from a concerned and loving partner now and plenty of social diversions to make for an interesting and stimulating Saturday. There are some distinct practical advantages about if you are willing to go out and look for them. Keep an open mind about new friendships.

22 SUNDAY
Moon Phase Day 28 • Moon Sign Scorpio

am ....

pm ....

The Sun takes a trip into your solar seventh house now, indicating that for the next month or so relationships are almost certain to play a much more important role in your life than will have been the case recently. Now is a good time to seek help of any sort, in the near certain knowledge that you will find it.

← NEGATIVE TREND						POSITIVE TREND →				
-5	-4	-3	-2	-1		+1	+2	+3	+4	+5
					LOVE					
					MONEY					
					LUCK					
					VITALITY					

23 MONDAY · *Moon Phase Day 29 • Moon Sign Scorpio*

am ....

pm ....

An almost mechanical feel to the day finds you getting things done at lightning speed, though perhaps not with the enthusiasm that is generally so much a part of your nature. You would be less than wise to think that you can solve all problems for yourself and should rely on the voice of wisdom that is close at hand.

24 TUESDAY · *Moon Phase Day 0 • Moon Sign Sagittarius*

am ....

pm ....

It is important that you allow other people to get their own way for a while, or at the very least to allow them to feel that they are doing so. Surprises abound on a social level and friends come good concerning promises that have been made for a while. You do need to recharge your batteries in an emotional sense.

25 WEDNESDAY · *Moon Phase Day 1• Moon Sign Sagittarius*

am ....

pm ....

The full force of the lunar low comes upon you today, even if you didn't really notice it lurking yesterday. That could be why you are feeling a little depleted and unable to cope with tasks that would generally give you very little trouble. Your capacity for work is undiminished however, and that might make you try too hard.

26 THURSDAY · *Moon Phase Day 2 • Moon Sign Capricorn*

am ....

pm ....

Nobody could deny the dutiful air that you are adopting now, though if you are only doing so for the sake of form, you might as well save yourself the bother. If you cannot do what is expected of you with a genuine desire to help, the whole thing is nothing more than a mockery; so have a think first!

27 FRIDAY
Moon Phase Day 3 • Moon Sign Capricorn

am ....

pm ....

A welcome release is found for present tensions, especially those that originate in your need to make the world exactly the place that you want it to be. Now you are much more inclined to accept what is on offer and not to tamper too much with circumstances. Memories come flooding back at some stage soon.

28 SATURDAY
Moon Phase Day 4 • Moon Sign Capricorn

am ....

pm ....

Allowing yourself to take the time to discover the lighter side of life again, after a rather sombre mood for a couple of days, you bring laughter not only into your own day but also into that of someone who is very dear to you. Items that you might have thought were lost for good suddenly begin to turn up again.

29 SUNDAY
Moon Phase Day 5 • Moon Sign Aquarius

am ....

pm ....

It is true that your self-image may take something of a knock today, probably because others don't display the picture of you that you thought they had. Perhaps you are not being as consistent as you should be and that could be part of the reason that you notice some resentment around you.

← *NEGATIVE TREND*   *POSITIVE TREND* →

-5	-4	-3	-2	-1		+1	+2	+3	+4	+5
					LOVE					
					MONEY					
					LUCK					
					VITALITY					

30 MONDAY

Moon Phase Day 6 • Moon Sign Aquarius

am ....

pm ....

The month ends with your dual personality really on display.' Who is this person that I know one day and find to be a stranger on the next?' This is a question that other people may be asking of you and it is very unlikely that you would be able to furnish them with an adequate answer because you don't know either!

1 TUESDAY

Moon Phase Day 7 • Moon Sign Pisces

am ....

pm ....

With the Sun now so firmly placed in your solar seventh house, the month opens bringing an air of importance to personal relationships on all levels. Loved ones are inclined to be rather pessimistic at present and will be turning to you for the support of your naturally cheerful and optimistic disposition.

2 WEDNESDAY

Moon Phase Day 8 • Moon Sign Pisces

am ....

pm ....

Spurred on by the way that you have been able to turn situations around for others, you now push your own incentives forward in a much more positive way and also reap the benefits of past actions. Home-comforts are more difficult to find than usual, though you could be too busy to notice.

3 THURSDAY

Moon Phase Day 9 • Moon Sign Pisces

am ....

pm ....

It really is a matter of keeping going at all costs, even with projects that bring doubts into your mind and make you wonder if you are really making any sense of things at all. Protect yourself against minor mishaps today by being especially careful and by refusing to take what you know to be unnecessary risks.

4 FRIDAY
Moon Phase Day 10 • Moon Sign Aries

am ....

pm ....

There are advantages to be gained from listening to your own inner mind today, especially if it is telling you that there is time and need for a rest. The practicalities of life can wait for the odd hour or two whilst you put your feet up. You have put sufficient effort in this week already.

5 SATURDAY
Moon Phase Day 11 • Moon Sign Aries

am ....

pm ....

Friends could prove to be a little tiresome, since they refuse to leave you alone and want you to solve all their problems for them. If they can't find you, this won't be so much of a problem and because you have every intention of keeping on the move, it won't be easy for them to pin you down.

6 SUNDAY
Moon Phase Day 12 • Moon Sign Taurus

am ....

pm ....

A particularly happy day in the deepest personal sense, with loved ones being extra considerate and surprise encounters proving to be of special interest. There are few clouds about to rain on your parade at present and just about the only irritation is likely to be your own slight lack of self-confidence.

← *NEGATIVE TREND*   *POSITIVE TREND* →

	-5	-4	-3	-2	-1		+1	+2	+3	+4	+5
LOVE								■			
MONEY							■				
LUCK											
VITALITY					■						

58

DECEMBER ♑
1992

YOUR MONTH AT A GLANCE

The twelve numbered boxes represent the important areas in your life. The key to the numbers you will find beneath the panel. A Sun above the number indicates that opportunities are around. A Cloud below the number, that you should be a bit defensive. Nothing above or below and life will be pretty ordinary.

1	2	3	4	5 ☀	6 ☀	7 ☀	8	9	10	11	12

KEY

1 Strength of Personality
2 Personal Finance
3 Useful Information Gathering
4 Domestic Affairs
5 Pleasure & Romance
6 Effective Work & Health

7 One to One Relationships
8 Questioning, Thinking & Deciding
9 External Influences / Education
10 Career Aspirations
11 Teamwork Activities
12 Unconscious Impulses

DECEMBER HIGHS AND LOWS

Here, I show how the rhythm of the Moon will affect you this month. Like the tide, your energies and abilities will rise and fall with its pattern. When it is above the date line, go-for-it. When it is below the line you should be resting.

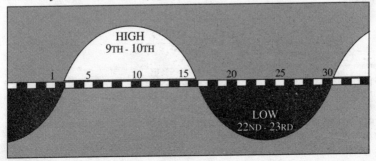

HIGH
9TH - 10TH

1   5   10   15   20   25   30

LOW
22ND - 23RD

59

7 MONDAY
Moon Phase Day 13 • Moon Sign Taurus

am ....

pm ....

Circumstances force you into a slightly more serious attitude to life today than you may otherwise be inclined to adopt. You will be moving heaven and earth to make things more comfortable for certain colleagues and might find a tendency to ingratitude difficult to deal with. Financially speaking, things run smoothly.

8 TUESDAY
Moon Phase Day 14 • Moon Sign Taurus

am ....

pm ....

It is more in a personal sense than in a fiscal one that you need to be on the lookout for some sort of double dealing on this Tuesday morning, despite the fact that there are also numerous people about who will be only too willing to do anything that they can for you. Avoid pointless over-reactions.

9 WEDNESDAY
Moon Phase Day 15 • Moon Sign Gemini

am ....

pm ....

Now that the lunar high pays you a visit again, you can look forward with confidence to a whole host of new possibilities that were never far from you in any case. Casting your mind forward towards Christmas, you should be laying down personal plans that can enable you to celebrate in greater comfort.

10 THURSDAY
Moon Phase Day 16 • Moon Sign Gemini

am ....

pm ....

Some slight gambles now begin to pay off and you also find that you are popular in a social sense too. With little to cloud your personal judgement, it is important that you also make your feelings known regarding the lives of your family, particularly someone who you know to have been going wrong.

60

11 FRIDAY

Moon Phase Day 17 • Moon Sign Cancer

am ....

pm ....

If you cannot find anything positive to say to people today, it might be better to say nothing at all. You won't be impressed by the hollow threats of an adversary, even in small matters, and will be more than willing to argue any point that you feel particularly strongly about at this time.

12 SATURDAY

Moon Phase Day 18 • Moon Sign Cancer

am ....

pm ....

You may not be at all sorry to see the weekend. It is fair to say that you can afford to allow responsibilities to take a back seat today and also let plans that you have laid down to simmer for a short while before you try to intervene again personally. A good day for all inconsequential matters.

13 SUNDAY

Moon Phase Day 19 • Moon Sign Leo

am ....

pm ....

Many laughs and a few groans of disbelief attend you today. You watch the antics of other people in slight disbelief, wondering how people could manage to get themselves into such a mess. Sooner or later you will have to help, though it wouldn't be wise to do so until you are asked!

14 MONDAY
Moon Phase Day 20 • Moon Sign Leo

am ....

pm ....

Leisure activities are high on your agenda now, not so surprising now that the festive season is so close. As always for Gemini folk, the advice is not to try and take on so much, thinking that you are immune to tiredness and pressure. This is especially true now that you are so busy at work.

15 TUESDAY
Moon Phase Day 21 • Moon Sign Virgo

am ....

pm ....

Ambitions rise and fall inside you, and in some ways you need a better definition of what life is all about as far as you personally are concerned. You work better when you have specific goals in mind and when you can encourage the sort of support that makes your own lot that much easier.

16 WEDNESDAY
Moon Phase Day 22 • Moon Sign Virgo

am ....

pm ....

If you are clever, you should be able to judge you own possible successes in a practical sense today simply by looking at the way one or two other people are managing their own lives. A few of you are so busy waging your own war against life that you fail to notice that the rest of the army has gone home.

17 THURSDAY
Moon Phase Day 23 • Moon Sign Libra

am ....

pm ....

A very rare phenomena is to find yourself working at anything alone, and this is as relevant to your social life as it would be in connection with your work. For once though, it appears that your own decisions suit you the best and that the involvement of friends and relatives makes for a temporary set-back.

18 FRIDAY
Moon Phase Day 24 • Moon Sign Libra

am ....

pm ....

You can't work out just why circumstances seem to be so set against you at present and so could keep knocking up against the same wall like some mechanical toy. Astrological influences favour flexibility now, so step back, have a think and then approach your destination from another direction.

19 SATURDAY
Moon Phase Day 25 • Moon Sign Scorpio

am ....

pm ....

Younger people come to the forefront of your life as a less self-possessed air takes you over for a number of days to come. The weekend is yours to enjoy, despite the fact that there are a number of practicalities to be dealt with and precious little time to spend on the situations that have real importance.

20 SUNDAY
Moon Phase Day 26 • Moon Sign Scorpio

am ....

pm ....

With depth and understanding, you can turn the tables on worry and kick it out of your life, for today at least. Irrational fears, so much a part of the Gemini thinking, are of very little importance now and it is the small, comic details of life that are apt to capture so much of your Sunday attention.

← *NEGATIVE TREND*   *POSITIVE TREND* →

-5	-4	-3	-2	-1		+1	+2	+3	+4	+5
					LOVE		▨			
				▨	MONEY					
					LUCK	▨				
					VITALITY	▨				

63

21 MONDAY

Moon Phase Day 27 • Moon Sign Scorpio

am ....

pm ....

Keep on the right side of your boss today and you can't go far wrong. Much is being expected of you, though it is the right part of the month to come out on top every time. It isn't only superiors who are in a position to help you because a close friend offers some timely advice too.

22 TUESDAY

Moon Phase Day 28 • Moon Sign Sagittarius

am ....

pm ....

A slight dip in spirits today is nothing more than a temporary setback and is really the legacy of the lunar low. It might be a bit of a bind finding yourself at this part of your personal lunar cycle so close to Christmas, though it only lasts a day or two and does allow you to stand back and look!

23 WEDNESDAY

Moon Phase Day 29 • Moon Sign Sagittarius

am ....

pm ....

Walking the streets looking into shop windows, or standing on a street corner and taking in the carols of the Sally Army band. Whatever you find the time to do, it is the sights and sounds of Christmas that really move you emotionally and offer the kind of thoughtful respite that you get all too rarely.

24 THURSDAY

Moon Phase Day 0 • Moon Sign Capricorn

am ....

pm ....

Back into the limelight and happy to be there, you charge into a thousand last-minute details with tremendous enthusiasm and not a little foolhardiness too! You are trying too hard, and remember, if you don't get to bed good and early tonight, Father Christmas is likely to give your house a miss!

25 FRIDAY
Moon Phase Day 1 • Moon Sign Capricorn

am ....

pm ....

A happy day, though you are left with the slight feeling of anti-climax, mainly because you always key yourself up too much in any case. Certain people are too willing to make a pass at you, and even though you could be flattered, there is some embarrassment too. What matters is that you keep a sense of proportion.

26 SATURDAY
Moon Phase Day 2 • Moon Sign Aquarius

am ....

pm ....

Strangely enough you may derive more personal pleasure from Boxing Day than you managed to find yesterday, perhaps because your personal expectations are fewer and the opportunities for mixing and mingling are greater. It should be possible to persuade other people to follow your line of reasoning.

27 SUNDAY
Moon Phase Day 3 • Moon Sign Aquarius

am ....

pm ....

Friends have some interesting and surprising news to impart. Whilst there are family members who could find time hanging heavy on their hands, nothing could be further from the truth as far as you are concerned, though you would definitely be at your best if allowed to go a-wandering at some stage during the day.

← NEGATIVE TREND							POSITIVE TREND →			
-5	-4	-3	-2	-1		+1	+2	+3	+4	+5
					LOVE					
					MONEY					
					LUCK					
					VITALITY					

28 MONDAY
Moon Phase Day 4 • Moon Sign Aquarius

am ....

pm ....

Draw a line under turmoil and problems from earlier parts of the year now that you are in frame of mind to really let go of excess baggage. This is particularly true in a personal sense, where some Gemini people have been registering emotional swings and a tendency to believe that past events might return.

29 TUESDAY
Moon Phase Day 5 • Moon Sign Pisces

am ....

pm ....

Still thinking a little more deeply than may be entirely good for you, it is at least possible to take stock, probably not entirely a bad thing as a year comes to an end. All the same there are things to be done and in nine cases out of ten at present it is you who will be called upon to take on the responsibility.

30 WEDNESDAY
Moon Phase Day 6 • Moon Sign Pisces

am ....

pm ....

It is the actions and general behaviour of other people that encourage you to lighten your own load prior to the end of a year that has treated you very well in the main. Don't look for perfection in anything today, you are not going to find it and can only frustrate yourself in the attempt.

31 THURSDAY
Moon Phase Day 7 • Moon Sign Aries

am ....

pm ....

As dynamic as you have been at any stage this month, you end the year in an optimistic and happy state, just right for casting your mind onward and upward to the excitement that always attends an unknown future as far as you are concerned. In a dispute that involves family and others, don't be too partisan.

1 FRIDAY
Moon Phase Day 8 • Moon Sign Aries

am ....

pm ....

The year of 1993 opens up for you on a very exciting note, with social arrangements uppermost in your mind and everything to play for in the days and weeks ahead. Press on with your plans in a professional sense and don't be distracted by negative people who have little or nothing of value to contribute.

2 SATURDAY
Moon Phase Day 9 • Moon Sign Aries

am ....

pm ....

Although it is very early in the year, the possibility of travel cannot be ruled out, and even if you are not actually stepping aboard the plane right at the moment, you could well be planning journeys for later. There is no doubt that you are in a restless frame of mind and respond well to changes of any sort now.

3 SUNDAY
Moon Phase Day 10 • Moon Sign Taurus

am ....

pm ....

Your own finances are boosted as, for once, your insist on getting good value for your money. In some ways you are more of a dark horse at present than usual, especially where your personal feelings are concerned. This might confuse others because they are used to you speaking out about anything and everything.

← *NEGATIVE TREND*						*POSITIVE TREND* →				
-5	-4	-3	-2	-1		+1	+2	+3	+4	+5
					LOVE					
					MONEY					
					LUCK					
					VITALITY					

JANUARY

1995

YOUR MONTH AT A GLANCE

The twelve numbered boxes represent the important areas in your life. The key to the numbers you will find beneath the panel. A Sun above the number indicates that opportunities are around. A Cloud below the number, that you should be a bit defensive. Nothing above or below and life will be pretty ordinary.

| 1 | 2 | 3 | 4 | 5 | 6 | 7 | 8 | 9 | 10 | 11 | 12 |

KEY

1 Strength of Personality
2 Personal Finance
3 Useful Information Gathering
4 Domestic Affairs
5 Pleasure & Romance
6 Effective Work & Health

7 One to One Relationships
8 Questioning, Thinking & Deciding
9 External Influences / Education
10 Career Aspirations
11 Teamwork Activities
12 Unconscious Impulses

JANUARY HIGHS AND LOWS

Here, I show how the rhythm of the Moon will affect you this month. Like the tide, your energies and abilities will rise and fall with its pattern. When it is above the date line, go-for-it. When it is below the line you should be resting.

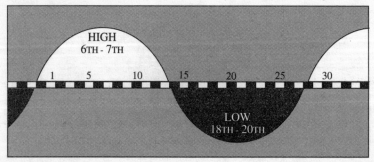

HIGH
6TH - 7TH

1   5   10   15   20   25   30

LOW
18TH - 20TH

4 MONDAY
Moon Phase Day11 • Moon Sign Taurus

am ....

pm ....

Things quieten down generally, though there is no doubt that you are deliberately opting for a steady way of going on as the new working week opens. Most individuals that you come across are affable enough and you only have to watch out for the odd person who appears to have a vested interest in putting you down.

5 TUESDAY
Moon Phase Day 12 • Moon Sign Taurus

am ....

pm ....

Energy levels are now definitely on the increase and it becomes possible to be more definite in both your ideas and your considered opinions. Perhaps this would be one of the few occasions this month when you could afford to take a calculated risk, as long as the odds are not too great.

6 WEDNESDAY
Moon Phase Day 13 • Moon Sign Gemini

am ....

pm ....

What sets this day apart as being quite special is the fact that it marks your lunar high, the two days or so each month when the Moon occupies your own zodiac sign and so is especially beneficial. With plenty of energy and an ever increasing belief in yourself, you have all the prerequisites of a fortunate day at your disposal.

7 THURSDAY
Moon Phase Day 14 • Moon Sign Gemini

am ....

pm ....

Some of the obstacles that really proved to be a problem to you towards the back end of last year are likely to be far less evident in your life now. Even strangers can be very useful in helping you to see personal matters more clearly, and the position of the Moon at the moment brings power to make necessary changes.

8 FRIDAY

Moon Phase Day 15 • Moon Sign Cancer

am ....

pm ....

The emphasis now is placed upon co-operative ventures and the sort of relationship that is truly of the sharing kind. If you think that it is time to sort out some particular aspect of your life that you are not especially happy with, the support that you require should be close at hand now, as long as you recognise it.

9 SATURDAY

Moon Phase Day 16 • Moon Sign Cancer

am ....

pm ....

The way that things have been working out in a personal sense may not have been exactly to your liking of late, which is why you might be choosing this time for a heart to heart talk with relatives or friends. Make it a relaxing weekend if you can, taking time out to be with the people whose company suits you the best.

10 SUNDAY

Moon Phase Day 17 • Moon Sign Leo

am ....

pm ....

News that finds its way to you now can act as a real eye opener and cause you to sit up and take notice of people that have not figured prominently in your life before. Levels of optimism and enthusiasm for life are high, which contribute to your cheerful personality and make special events go with a swing.

← NEGATIVE TREND								POSITIVE TREND →				
-5	-4	-3	-2	-1			+1	+2	+3	+4	+5
					LOVE						
					MONEY						
					LUCK						
					VITALITY						

YOUR DAILY GUIDE TO JANUARY 1993

11 MONDAY — Moon Phase Day 18 • Moon Sign Leo

am ....

pm ....

Planetary aspects today serve to emphasise the value that other
people have to your life at the present time. Friendship is especially
important and one or two people especially begin to play a much
more important role in your day to day decision making. Take care
over expenditure as money could be in relatively short supply.

12 TUESDAY — Moon Phase Day 19 • Moon Sign Virgo

am ....

pm ....

You ought to have something to feel excited about, though it is likely
that you just can't think of anything off hand. It is quite important
to express yourself in very certain terms, allowing other people to
realise that you have some very strong opinions. This should lead to
further discussions and acts as a necessary stimulus to you.

13 WEDNESDAY — Moon Phase Day 20 • Moon Sign Virgo

am ....

pm ....

Getting priorities right in a domestic sense may not be too easy and
that could lead to arguments with people who presently have a very
different set of opinions to the ones that you hold to. Matters that
are closest to your heart are not always easy to talk about, even for
you, so seek out a particularly sympathetic friend.

14 THURSDAY — Moon Phase Day 21 • Moon Sign Libra

am ....

pm ....

The swings of the Gemini nature are legendary and you should find
that any reservations or quietness of nature left over from yesterday
is soon dissipated as you become busy with a host of new projects
now. Your general attitude is more decisive, making it easier for
others to know what it is you are seeking.

15 FRIDAY

Moon Phase Day 22 • Moon Sign Libra

am ....

pm ....

It would be very wise to avert your gaze from the unattainable, both in a personal and a materialistic sense, at the present time. It isn't possible to have everything that you want in your life, and even where it is, the price that you sometimes have to pay is far too high. Be wise and count your present blessings.

16 SATURDAY

Moon Phase Day 23 • Moon Sign Scorpio

am ....

pm ....

Confidence boosters come along in the form of kind words, possibly of a romantic nature. You could be quite surprised by the opinions that proliferate in your immediate circle, though you are less likely than usual to add your own rather unique contribution to most debates for the next couple of days at least.

17 SUNDAY

Moon Phase Day 24 • Moon Sign Scorpio

am ....

pm ....

The position of Mercury in particular ensures that you are in a carefree and particularly high spirited frame of mind, even if you are not expressing your opinions in quite the way that people are used to hearing them. Don't expect this day to be especially productive, it's important that you have the time to simply look around for once.

NEGATIVE TREND						POSITIVE TREND				
-5	-4	-3	-2	-1		+1	+2	+3	+4	+5
					LOVE					
					MONEY					
					LUCK					
					VITALITY					

18 MONDAY   *Moon Phase Day 25 • Moon Sign Sagittarius*

am ....

pm ....

As the Moon occupies your opposite sign of Sagittarius, you find that
the lunar low for the month tends to sap your energy and prevents
you from bringing your usual enthusiasm to bear on life. You may
choose to stay away from social gatherings and will prefer the company of your nearest and dearest once work is out of the way.

19 TUESDAY   *Moon Phase Day 26 • Moon Sign Sagittarius*

am ....

pm ....

Still resting and recharging those overworked Gemini batteries, you
are now able to stand back and take stock of many aspects of your
life that you don't normally have the chance to look at closely. This
is the main benefit of the lunar low, forcing even the perpetual mo-
tion of your sign to resign itself to less demanding patterns.

20 WEDNESDAY   *Moon Phase Day 27 • Moon Sign Sagittarius*

am ....

pm ....

As the first of your lunar low periods of the year begins to fade in
strength, you should discover that it leaves you feeling far more settled in yourself than you may have expected to be. People are turning to you for the sort of advice that is easy to offer, but which is of
tremendous importance as far as they are concerned.

21 THURSDAY   *Moon Phase Day 28 • Moon Sign Capricorn*

am ....

pm ....

Restless now, and anxious for the sort of new experiences that you
probably feel have been eluding you recently, you cast around for
new situations to take up the slack in your constantly churning
mind. The busy pace of your professional life can open all sorts of
new doors, though you will need to keep a check on available time.

22 FRIDAY
Moon Phase Day 0 • Moon Sign Capricorn

am ....

pm ....

Outside of work it should be possible to find a fulfilling social life just at the moment, and there are plenty of people about to offer you the sort of company that pleases you the best. Be as open as you can to all new ideas, particularly of the sort that you can work on and improve in the months ahead.

23 SATURDAY
Moon Phase Day 1 • Moon Sign Aquarius

am ....

pm ....

Now your views are very strong and you regain the verbal dexterity to put them across quite forcefully. What might be somewhat frustrating is the fact that other people are so affected by the power of your speech that they fail to disagree with you, or even to express an opinion at all in some cases.

24 SUNDAY
Moon Phase Day 2 • Moon Sign Aquarius

am ....

pm ....

If you really want to make the sort of general progress that you have been looking for, especially in a personal sense, you are going to have to turn the tact up to full volume and also take notice of what others have to say. This may not be as easy as it sounds, since you are quite adamant in most opinions at the present time.

← NEGATIVE TREND						POSITIVE TREND →				
-5	-4	-3	-2	-1		+1	+2	+3	+4	+5
					LOVE					
					MONEY					
					LUCK					
					VITALITY					

25 MONDAY   *Moon Phase Day 3 • Moon Sign Aquarius*

am ....

pm ....

All professional and personal considerations are about to receive a boost, allowing you the chance to feel that things are really going the way that you would want them to do. It is important to be patient where some of your cherished professional plans are concerned, though there is plenty to keep you occupied for now.

26 TUESDAY   *Moon Phase Day 4 • Moon Sign Pisces*

am ....

pm ....

Life goes on in fits and starts just now; not exactly a desirable state of affairs but one that is quite common to the lives of Gemini individuals. It is important to sort out which aspects of your schedule you ought to be concentrating on and push other, less important matters to the back of your mind.

27 WEDNESDAY   *Moon Phase Day 5 • Moon Sign Pisces*

am ....

pm ....

Away from the confines of your work, which can be very stifling at the present time, you should be happy to seek out and discover a particularly rewarding period socially. Now is the time to reward yourself for the successes of the recent past and to take some time out from boring routines to really shine in company.

28 THURSDAY   *Moon Phase Day 6 • Moon Sign Aries*

am ....

pm ....

Back in the swing of practicalities, there is little doubt that other people set you apart in some way and probably also treat you with a respect that you haven't been used to in the recent past. You are in an ideal position to see things clearly though and can be relied upon to work methodically towards the needs that others have of you.

29 FRIDAY
Moon Phase Day 7 • Moon Sign Aries

am ....

pm ....

The planetary emphasis is quite clearly on social and personal matters. With the weekend coming up you should be giving some thought to ways of amusing yourself, whilst at the same time finding the means to keep those closest to you happy too. People who have had deep troubles find you good to have around right now.

30 SATURDAY
Moon Phase Day 8 • Moon Sign Aries

am ....

pm ....

There is likely to be a slight lull in the break-neck routines that have been so much a part of the last few days. Although you take it on yourself to entertain everyone that you come across, it would be good to make certain that you get at least a little time to yourself and are not constantly being found something to do.

31 SUNDAY
Moon Phase Day 9 • Moon Sign Taurus

am ....

pm ....

Stay away from differences of opinion that have nothing to do with you because it wouldn't be at all advisable to become involved in personal disputes at the present time. Despite your reticence to be drawn into matters that are not of your own making, you will be prepared to tackle some crucial decisions, as long as you have all the facts.

← NEGATIVE TREND								POSITIVE TREND →			
-5	-4	-3	-2	-1			+1	+2	+3	+4	+5
					LOVE						
					MONEY						
					LUCK						
					VITALITY						

FEBRUARY
1993

YOUR MONTH AT A GLANCE

The twelve numbered boxes represent the important areas in your life. The key to the numbers you will find beneath the panel. A Sun above the number indicates that opportunities are around. A Cloud below the number, that you should be a bit defensive. Nothing above or below and life will be pretty ordinary.

1	2	3	4	5	6	7	8	9	10	11	12

KEY

1 Strength of Personality	7 One to One Relationships
2 Personal Finance	8 Questioning, Thinking & Deciding
3 Useful Information Gathering	9 External Influences / Education
4 Domestic Affairs	10 Career Aspirations
5 Pleasure & Romance	11 Teamwork Activities
6 Effective Work & Health	12 Unconscious Impulses

FEBRUARY HIGHS AND LOWS

Here, I show how the rhythm of the Moon will affect you this month. Like the tide, your energies and abilities will rise and fall with its pattern. When it is above the date line, go-for-it. When it is below the line you should be resting.

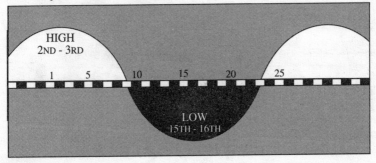

HIGH
2ND - 3RD

1   5   10   15   20   25

LOW
15TH - 16TH

1 MONDAY
Moon Phase Day 10 • Moon Sign Taurus

am ....

pm ....

The start of February is quite fortunate since you are on the verge of your monthly lunar high, a fact that is hardly likely to go unheeded, when the possible benefits tumble over themselves in an effort to get to you. You should be feeling very lucky and can afford to take some calculated risks, as long as you exercise a little care.

2 TUESDAY
Moon Phase Day 11 • Moon Sign Gemini

am ....

pm ....

Finding yourself in the midst of a light hearted atmosphere, you will be doing your best to contribute to proceedings in any way that you can. People find you good to have around and will be indulging your sense of fun. In routine matters it is quite easy to get your own way and to talk others round to your point of view.

3 WEDNESDAY
Moon Phase Day 12 • Moon Sign Gemini

am ....

pm ....

The lunar high is still having the most important bearing on the type of circumstances that surround you at present and leads you into the path of very useful new contacts in a personal and professional sense. Associates can become good friends in the days ahead and your general circle is growing all the time.

4 THURSDAY
Moon Phase Day 13 • Moon Sign Cancer

am ....

pm ....

The need to discuss finances with the people who are also affected by your actions, though to do so could lead to a situation of confrontation that might be avoided altogether with just a little tact all round. Of course you cannot tell others how they should behave but you don't have to rise to their bait unless you wish to do so.

5 FRIDAY
Moon Phase Day 14 • Moon Sign Cancer

am ....

pm ....

Promises that have been made to you are inclined to be late materialising, if they do so at all! This is a period when patience would be a deciding factor, though you don't come from the most patient part of the zodiac and could be just a little short tempered in any case. As far as progress at work in concerned, things are better.

6 SATURDAY
Moon Phase Day 15 • Moon Sign Leo

am ....

pm ....

There is no doubting that your powers of communication were forged within the planet Mercury and you could truly talk the hind leg off the proverbial donkey at the present time. This gift is especially useful at a time when you may be looking at the possibility of new interests developing in your life.

7 SUNDAY
Moon Phase Day 16 • Moon Sign Leo

am ....

pm ....

A serious 'back to basics' approach is required with regard to things that need doing at home. All the same, don't concentrate on practical situations to the exclusion of all else. You have the ability to lift someone out of a deep depression now; all you have to do is to turn on the clowning and make them laugh.

← *NEGATIVE TREND*   *POSITIVE TREND* →

-5	-4	-3	-2	-1		+1	+2	+3	+4	+5
					LOVE					
					MONEY					
					LUCK					
					VITALITY					

8 MONDAY
Moon Phase Day 17 • Moon Sign Virgo

am ....

pm ....

There are chances for advancement now that may have been a closed book to you in the past for one reason or another. In fact it is possible that you may discover what it is that has been prejudicing your chances in the past. Such knowledge could anger you but there is no reason to react violently as a result.

9 TUESDAY
Moon Phase Day 18 • Moon Sign Virgo

am ....

pm ....

Once again your greatest skill comes in the direction of bringing others round to what you would consider to be a sensible point of view. Friends are loving and caring, just right for you to be asking one or two favours of them that they would be unlikely to deny you now. Colleagues rely on your 'softly softly' approach.

10 WEDNESDAY
Moon Phase Day 19 • Moon Sign Libra

am ....

pm ....

Could it be that you have a secret admirer somewhere? It looks that way at the moment, though typical of your sign and despite your normally intuitive nature, you could be the last one to realise the fact. Romance figures largely at this time, even for Geminis who are more than settled in a permanent relationship. There are a wealth of

11 THURSDAY
Moon Phase Day 20 • Moon Sign Libra

am ....

pm ....

stubborn and very narrow-minded people about, who you will have to deal with in the near future. It is amazing how much the Gemini nature acts as a mirror to stimuli that come in from outside and, true to this fact, you are certain to be just as stubborn as the individuals you are presented with.

12 FRIDAY
Moon Phase Day 21 • Moon Sign Scorpio

am ....

pm ....

With the present relative positions of the Sun and Mercury, you are not likely to be in everyone's good books at the present time, despite the fact that in a number of cases you don't really understand why. It is very necessary to take their feeling into account if you can and it would be an idea to try and find out what you might have done.

13 SATURDAY
Moon Phase Day 22 • Moon Sign Scorpio

am ....

pm ....

Life in a general sense is probably slowing down to a pace that seems to be especially slow, despite the fact that it does your sign good to realise that you can't be reacting to exciting events all the time. Because it is the weekend you will be doing all you can to speed up those elements of your routines that you can control.

14 SUNDAY
Moon Phase Day 23 • Moon Sign Scorpio

am ....

pm ....

Things are still likely to be fairly quiet and you find yourself in an interlude which demands you being the catalyst for any changes or excitement that might be possible. Don't take the things that other people have to say to you at face value, being prepared to take all 'tall tales' as being an approximation of the truth.

← NEGATIVE TREND							POSITIVE TREND →			
-5	-4	-3	-2	-1		+1	+2	+3	+4	+5
					LOVE					
					MONEY					
					LUCK					
					VITALITY					

15 MONDAY   *Moon Phase Day 24 • Moon Sign Sagittarius*

am ....

pm ....

The lunar low certainly does have a dampening role to play, forcing you to look and plan, without necessarily actually doing a great deal. Confusion can arise in a personal sense, with misunderstandings at home being the backbone of the problem. Some extra patience and understanding would seem to be called for.

16 TUESDAY   *Moon Phase Day 25 • Moon Sign Sagittarius*

am ....

pm ....

As the Moon steams away from your opposite sign later in the day you are likely to breathe a sigh of relief without really understanding why. Almost immediately the grass looks greener and the sky more blue. Restlessness can be controlled as the day wears on but it isn't likely that you can prevent it altogether.

17 WEDNESDAY   *Moon Phase Day 26 • Moon Sign Capricorn*

am ....

pm ....

You find that the 'pendulum effect', so common in the lives of mercurial Geminis, comes into play now, particularly where financial prospects are concerned. One minute it appears that there is more cash around than you expected and the next you are on the receiving end of demands for payment. Things soon improve.

18 THURSDAY   *Moon Phase Day 27 • Moon Sign Capricorn*

am ....

pm ....

There certainly isn't sufficient time to undertake everything that you would wish to do at the moment so it is vitally important to take an inventory of outstanding tasks and approach them in order of importance. Life is still a little up and down in most respects, particularly if you don't get sufficient rest.

19 FRIDAY   *Moon Phase Day 28 • Moon Sign Aquarius*

am ....

pm ....

At the end of a fairly mediocre working week, all your chickens come home to roost at the same time, though in a very positive and potentially lucrative way. It isn't what you are doing at the moment that really counts but what you have accomplished in the past. Be prepared to be recognised as the clever person that you truly are.

20 SATURDAY   *Moon Phase Day 29 • Moon Sign Aquarius*

am ....

pm ....

Variety and change are of utmost importance now that Saturday is here. The weather may not be brilliant but there is still a need for you to get out and about, if possible visiting friends and making the most of any entertaining company that is available. Encourage family members not to live in your pocket.

21 SUNDAY   *Moon Phase Day 0 • Moon Sign Aquarius*

am ....

pm ....

News comes in from far away, and nobody loves to hear of distant places with strange sounding names more than you do. Pressure is lifted slightly in a personal sense and relationships appear to run more smoothly than has been possible for a while past. Look to this week for an improvement of financial rewards.

← *NEGATIVE TREND*   *POSITIVE TREND* →

-5	-4	-3	-2	-1		+1	+2	+3	+4	+5
					LOVE	▓	▓			
					MONEY	▓				
					LUCK	▓				
				▓	VITALITY					

22 MONDAY

Moon Phase Day 1 • Moon Sign Pisces

am ....

pm ....

The way that you are thinking about reorganising your working life could turn out to be a key to greater success than you ever imagined. It is relatively easy to keep well abreast of the changes that take place in events and to make allowances for them. Domestic situations also bring their own rewards as the days pass.

23 TUESDAY

Moon Phase Day 2 • Moon Sign Pisces

am ....

pm ....

People are responsible for a great deal of mischief, much of which is likely to rebound in your direction unless you keep your wits about you and stay ahead of the game. Social meetings are pleasurable and help to pass some happy hours. Practically speaking, most aspects of life are apt to sort themselves out now.

24 WEDNESDAY

Moon Phase Day 3 • Moon Sign Aries

am ....

pm ....

Take a listening approach in all your involvement with other people, especially in a work setting. Disagreements with colleagues are almost certain to occur but shouldn't be taken as being anything more than an interlude that will pass quickly enough if you don't pay them too much attention.

25 THURSDAY

Moon Phase Day 4 • Moon Sign Aries

am ....

pm ....

Lighten the atmosphere socially as often as you can now, and make certain that you listen carefully, not only to what people are saying but also to what isn't being said. Your partner is likely to be especially helpful and understanding, leading to a more romantic period and an extra effort on your part to show how much you appreciate your life.

26 FRIDAY
Moon Phase Day 5 • Moon Sign Aries

am ....

pm ....

Life finds means and ways of putting you through your paces, not that you are concerned because it always does you good to flex your intellectual muscles as well as your physical ones. As far as friends are concerned, your sympathies are easily roused and you will want to do all that you can to help them out of a jam.

27 SATURDAY
Moon Phase Day 6 • Moon Sign Taurus

am ....

pm ....

Perhaps it is your present attentive manner, or maybe just that life is running fairly smoothly all round at the moment. Whatever the cause you have the basis of an extremely happy Sunday at your disposal, though of course what you choose to make of it in reality depends upon you. Emotional needs bring out the best in you.

28 SUNDAY
Moon Phase Day 7 • Moon Sign Taurus

am ....

pm ....

Officials and authority figures may have the upper hand today and there is probably no point at all in arguing. Bide your time and wait patiently because you are certain to get what is fair in the long-run. Think through all practical and professional matters as carefully as you can before taking any decisive action.

← *NEGATIVE TREND*   *POSITIVE TREND* →

-5	-4	-3	-2	-1		+1	+2	+3	+4	+5
					LOVE					
					MONEY					
					LUCK					
					VITALITY					

MARCH
1993

YOUR MONTH AT A GLANCE

The twelve numbered boxes represent the important areas in your life.
The key to the numbers you will find beneath the panel. A Sun above
the number indicates that opportunities are around. A Cloud below
the number, that you should be a bit defensive. Nothing above or
below and life will be pretty ordinary.

1	2	3	4	5	6	7	8	9	10	11	12

KEY

1 Strength of Personality	7 One to One Relationships
2 Personal Finance	8 Questioning, Thinking & Deciding
3 Useful Information Gathering	9 External Influences / Education
4 Domestic Affairs	10 Career Aspirations
5 Pleasure & Romance	11 Teamwork Activities
6 Effective Work & Health	12 Unconscious Impulses

MARCH HIGHS AND LOWS

Here, I show how the rhythm of the Moon will affect you this month.
Like the tide, your energies and abilities will rise and fall with its pattern. When it is above the date line, go-for-it. When it is below the
line you should be resting.

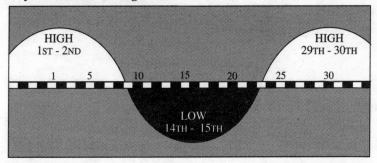

HIGH
1ST - 2ND

HIGH
29TH - 30TH

1   5   10   15   20   25   30

LOW
14TH - 15TH

1 MONDAY
Moon Phase Day 8 • Moon Sign Gemini

am ....

pm ....

Starting the month with a sudden burst of energy, you probably will not be surprised to learn that the lunar high is around. It is now easy to initiate some important changes in your working life, in the certain knowledge that you have your facts right and that there are plenty of people around who are willing to lend a hand.

2 TUESDAY
Moon Phase Day 9 • Moon Sign Gemini

am ....

pm ....

Being especially receptive to the needs of the people around you, not only friends but business associates too, there is little surprise that you find yourself in demand. Another favourable day for getting what you want in a professional sense and a continuation of the help that you have been receiving from friends is sure to be welcome.

3 WEDNESDAY
Moon Phase Day 10 • Moon Sign Gemini

am ....

pm ....

The spotlight falls on practical situations, as you manage to deal with a mass of difficult situations with impunity. At the same time you could experience some obstacles regarding long-term plans and need to keep your options open and your mind on the future. Information received can be of tremendous importance.

4 THURSDAY
Moon Phase Day 11• Moon Sign Cancer

am ....

pm ....

As some of the success begins to fade, it would be difficult not to imagine that the grass looks greener on the other side of the fence, especially in a professional sense. All the same, you have to realise that short interludes such as this are inevitable from time to time and shouldn't be used as an excuse to slacken your efforts.

5 FRIDAY
Moon Phase Day 12 • Moon Sign Cancer

am ....

pm ....

Because you are now willing and able to speak your mind, at home as well as at work, you are more in command and able to make sense of situations that were more complicated to fathom yesterday. Old patterns of thinking will have to be looked at again and though it isn't always easy to change, you stand a better chance than most.

6 SATURDAY
Moon Phase Day 13 • Moon Sign Cancer

am ....

pm ....

Most sons and daughters of Mercury will be more than happy to welcome the arrival of this weekend, even though things are looking quite rosy. The problem is that you have never learned how to give seventy per cent of yourself instead of a hundred to anything and consequently wear yourself out as a result. Take some rest now.

7 SUNDAY
Moon Phase Day 14 • Moon Sign Leo

am ....

pm ....

Your partner or a family member is more than willing to make a sacrifice or two on your behalf, not that you are asking them to do so. This should be a real family day and one that offers the chance to do something completely out of the ordinary. It can't be denied that in the life of any Gemini, a change is as good as a rest.

← NEGATIVE TREND										
-5	-4	-3	-2	-1		+1	+2	+3	+4	+5
					LOVE					
					MONEY					
					LUCK					
					VITALITY					

POSITIVE TREND →

8 MONDAY
Moon Phase Day 15 • Moon Sign Virgo

am ....

pm ....

At the back of your mind is a great desire for and an expectation of change. What this is likely to represent as far as you are concerned remains to be seen, though your intuition is strong and so your hunch is certain to be correct. Don't try to influence circumstances too much now but let life 'flow' for you.

9 TUESDAY
Moon Phase Day 16 • Moon Sign Virgo

am ....

pm ....

Other people may be doing their best but they are unlikely to match up to your expectations in the days ahead, and that could mean that you feel yourself pressured into doing more than is good for you. You have to learn that you can't take on the responsibilities of the world, no matter how much you might wish to.

10 WEDNESDAY
Moon Phase Day 17 • Moon Sign Libra

am ....

pm ....

Present planetary aspects indicate a shift in emphasis for a day or two, away from the more practical aspects of your life and towards personal attachments, the implications of which take up a far greater percentage of your time than they have done recently. Leisure interests undertaken now can bring enormous advantages.

11 THURSDAY
Moon Phase Day 18 • Moon Sign Libra

am ....

pm ....

The working week grinds on, perhaps without your customary optimism for a day or two. It could appear that many of your efforts have led to nothing, despite the fact that you are inclined not to wait long enough before you begin to get depressed about things. Consider situations to be on ice and not lost.

12 FRIDAY
Moon Phase Day 19 • Moon Sign Scorpio

am ....

pm ....

Once again there is a shift in emphasis, away from the present slightly grey shades of practical living and towards the possibilities that are evident in an entertainment sense. It may be the end of the working week for you, which works well alongside the present position of Mercury to make you expert at cheering up other people.

13 SATURDAY
Moon Phase Day 20 • Moon Sign Scorpio

am ....

pm ....

Although you are still full of beans in every sense, there are strong indications that things generally are about to slow down noticeably. The better weather and longer days indicate the approach of Spring and could mean that you would gain personally from getting out and about during the weekend. Friends gather around you.

14 SUNDAY
Moon Phase Day 21 • Moon Sign Sagittarius

am ....

pm ....

Finding that your energy levels are still slipping, you may not be too surprised to discover that the Moon is now in your opposite sign, bringing the lunar low back into your life. There is nothing to prevent activities that promote rest and recuperation, so there is little reason why you shouldn't still be enjoying a weekend of outings.

← NEGATIVE TREND							POSITIVE TREND →			
-5	-4	-3	-2	-1		+1	+2	+3	+4	+5
					LOVE					
					MONEY					
					LUCK					
					VITALITY					

15 MONDAY
Moon Phase Day 22 • Moon Sign Sagittarius

am ....

pm ....

Not everything that you do must have an end product or an ulterior motive, a fact that is easier to come to terms with at a time when circumstances hold you back in any case. Plod on slowly and steadily, doing those things that are expected of you but taking time out to watch the flowers grow while you are about it.

16 TUESDAY
Moon Phase Day 23 • Moon Sign Capricorn

am ....

pm ....

With the Sun and Pluto now forming a particularly positive aspect as far as you are concerned, personal prospects begin to look more settled again. Some of the restlessness which has beset you recently fades and you find it less difficult to concentrate on the job in hand. Superiors are taking notice of your unique ideas.

17 WEDNESDAY
Moon Phase Day 24 • Moon Sign Capricorn

am ....

pm ....

In a brighter world today, your natural curiosity is being stimulated to a greater degree and you look with fascination and wonder at a world that rarely ceases to amaze you. Even when other people countermand your instructions you are likely to look for the reason rather than becoming upset by the eventuality.

18 THURSDAY
Moon Phase Day 25• Moon Sign Capricorn

am ....

pm ....

Romance begins to flourish and you make a special fuss of the one that you love the most. In many of the ways that count you are good to have around and are doing all that you can to stimulate your own sense of happiness in people who may be less fortunate than yourself. Some restlessness returns, though probably not for long.

19 FRIDAY
Moon Phase Day 26 • Moon Sign Aquarius

am ....

pm ....

You can't really avoid looking on the blacker side of life if that is the way that circumstances line themselves up at the present time, though you won't have any desire to dwell in dark realms for longer than you have to. Perhaps it is the negative attitudes of others that force you into being more pensive.

20 SATURDAY
Moon Phase Day 27 • Moon Sign Aquarius

am ....

pm ....

With opposition being expressed, probably concerning plans that you have for changes on the home front, you are quite willing to be a democrat as long as all the votes go in your favour. Nevertheless, you won't achieve a lot by trying to bulldoze your plans through and must take some time out to persuade.

21 SUNDAY
Moon Phase Day 28 • Moon Sign Pisces

am ....

pm ....

In a period of greater social involvement, there are causes to look for and situations that respond to your special skills and sense of timing. Rewards that are attainable won't necessarily be exclusively ones that have a bearing on you personally, though the happiness that you can help to bring to others does please you.

← *NEGATIVE TREND*   *POSITIVE TREND* →

-5	-4	-3	-2	-1		+1	+2	+3	+4	+5
					LOVE					
					MONEY					
					LUCK					
					VITALITY					

22 MONDAY
Moon Phase Day 29 • Moon Sign Pisces

am ....

pm ....

Once you have decided on a particular course of action at the present time you are far less likely to be diverted or side-tracked than would usually be the case. This kind of determination is not something that you would usually notice in your day to day nature but it does ensure that things get done efficiently.

23 TUESDAY
Moon Phase Day 0 • Moon Sign Pisces

am ....

pm ....

There is a chance that you could get ahead at the expense of other people, a situation that you are unlikely to take advantage of unless you know that third parties are likely to benefit too. Loved ones tend to pull you back and forth in an emotional sense, which doesn't do much to make you any more settled.

24 WEDNESDAY
Moon Phase Day 1 • Moon Sign Aries

am ....

pm ....

Peace and quiet, together with the warmth of familiar surroundings, really appears to have an appeal all of its own at the present time. This could be a slight return of your sense of insecurity so does need to be countered a little. Of course there is nothing wrong with rest for its own sake.

25 THURSDAY
Moon Phase Day 2 • Moon Sign Aries

am ....

pm ....

Keep a careful eye on finances because there should be just enough about at the moment but not a great deal more. This would not be a good time for speculation because your hunches are less likely to pay off and some of the things that you see as being golden opportunities turn out to be anything but.

26 FRIDAY
Moon Phase Day 3• Moon Sign Taurus

am ....

pm ....

Now you embark upon an intensely personal period, when decisions must be made with regard to relationships and what they have to offer you in the medium and long-term sense. You might think that your present way of thinking is a little selfish but there is nothing wrong with wanting to get your life in order.

27 SATURDAY
Moon Phase Day 4 • Moon Sign Taurus

am ....

pm ....

Past matters are just that, and shouldn't be treated as a cause for major concern at the the present time. Doubtless you appear to be more moody than would usually be the case but remember that nothing lasts long in the life of the Gemini and that you can bounce back in a moment if the opportunity to do so arises.

28 SUNDAY
Moon Phase Day 5 • Moon Sign Taurus

am ....

pm ....

For the second time within a month, the fast moving Moon draws close to your own Sun-sign and is able to lift you above yourself in a way that makes an over-view of your life easy to achieve. Take good advice at any stage that you recognise it as such and marvel at the generous behaviour of your friends.

← NEGATIVE TREND								POSITIVE TREND →			
-5	-4	-3	-2	-1			+1	+2	+3	+4	+5
					LOVE						
					MONEY						
					LUCK						
					VITALITY						

29 MONDAY
Moon Phase Day 6 • Moon Sign Gemini

am ....

pm ....

General levels of luck are on the increase, though sadly this doesn't mean that you are in a position to put your shirt on the first horse that looks as if it might stay the course. This sort of luck has far more to do with events than money, and can help to put you in the right place at the right time.

30 TUESDAY
Moon Phase Day 7 • Moon Sign Gemini

am ....

pm ....

Your love life can be challenging in some way now, perhaps because the way that your mind is working doesn't exactly conform to that of your partner. This is an opportunity to prove how flexible you can be, and shows just how fair you really are when opinions other than your own are expressed close to home.

31 WEDNESDAY
Moon Phase Day 8 • Moon Sign Cancer

am ....

pm ....

The month ends on a comfort seeking note for you. Despite any workaday pressures that might be forced upon you, it is the period after work that turns out to be the most important. With disputes now settled and the warmth of a loving embrace more important to you, you revel in the simple pleasures of your domain.

1 THURSDAY
Moon Phase Day 9 • Moon Sign Cancer

am ....

pm ....

There may be some April Fools about at the present time, though except in the sense of playing the fool willingly you are not likely to be one of them. This could be a high spot as far as social gatherings are concerned and makes demands upon your time. Still, the happiness that you help to create is well worth the effort.

2 FRIDAY
Moon Phase Day 10 • Moon Sign Leo

am ....

pm ....

Intense emotional involvement cannot be avoided at the present time, but it can and should be toned down if you want to avoid turning yourself inside out. Stick to practical considerations and clear the decks, ready for the weekend. Many of your instructions seem to be ignored.

3 SATURDAY
Moon Phase Day 11 • Moon Sign Leo

am ....

pm ....

Pressures upon you appear to demand an especially decisive approach to life on your part, so it is a good job that you have more sense than to fall for rumours and hearsay. Plod along in your own sweet way and do your best to make certain that the weekend is different in some way.

4 SUNDAY
Moon Phase Day 12 • Moon Sign Virgo

am ....

pm ....

Where family matters appear to give you more cause for concern than you think is really justified by the way that circumstances are proceeding, tread lightly and wait to see what the next couple of days might bring in the way of alterations. Meanwhile, keep ringing the changes and be totally honest with friends.

← *NEGATIVE TREND*								*POSITIVE TREND* →		
-5	-4	-3	-2	-1		+1	+2	+3	+4	+5
					LOVE					
					MONEY					
					LUCK					
					VITALITY					

APRIL 1993

YOUR MONTH AT A GLANCE

The twelve numbered boxes represent the important areas in your life. The key to the numbers you will find beneath the panel. A Sun above the number indicates that opportunities are around. A Cloud below the number, that you should be a bit defensive. Nothing above or below and life will be pretty ordinary.

1	2	3	4	5	6	7	8	9	10	11	12

KEY

1 Strength of Personality
2 Personal Finance
3 Useful Information Gathering
4 Domestic Affairs
5 Pleasure & Romance
6 Effective Work & Health

7 One to One Relationships
8 Questioning, Thinking & Deciding
9 External Influences / Education
10 Career Aspirations
11 Teamwork Activities
12 Unconscious Impulses

APRIL HIGHS AND LOWS

Here, I show how the rhythm of the Moon will affect you this month. Like the tide, your energies and abilities will rise and fall with its pattern. When it is above the date line, go-for-it. When it is below the line you should be resting.

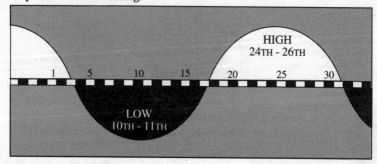

HIGH
24TH - 26TH

LOW
10TH - 11TH

5 MONDAY   *Moon Phase Day 13 • Moon Sign Virgo*

am ....

pm ....

Light relief comes into your life, not only from the direction of friends but also because of colleagues and acquaintances. You shouldn't have to look too far to find genuine affection, there are people about who admire and care for you that are perhaps unwilling to admit how deep their feelings go.

6 TUESDAY   *Moon Phase Day 14 • Moon Sign Libra*

am ....

pm ....

Mentally and even in a physical sense, most Geminis should be on an all time high. Some misuse of the trust that you have been willing to put in other people could bring one or two minor disappointments, though if anything you find yourself in the midst of a generally uneventful period.

7 WEDNESDAY   *Moon Phase Day 15 • Moon Sign Libra*

am ....

pm ....

Look out for financial propositions, which are likely to be especially favourable if viewed and dealt with at this point in time. The middle of the week could spell anything but contentment in a workaday sense, probably because you are feeling restless in any case. It is hard to be patient at this time.

8 THURSDAY   *Moon Phase Day 16 • Moon Sign Scorpio*

am ....

pm ....

Even if you do have the occasional doubt at the present time, it is very unlikely that you will change your mind. Despite the fact that there are dozens of people around you, all of whom are convinced that they know better than you do, stick to your own guns and behave as you think fit.

9 FRIDAY

Moon Phase Day 17 • Moon Sign Scorpio

am ....

pm ....

Crowded in by responsibility and held back by the negative ideas that almost everyone you meet appears to have, you would hardly expect this to be the most fortunate day of the month. You might be right, but that doesn't mean that there are no gains to be made at all. Take an hour or two to yourself and have a ponder.

10 SATURDAY

Moon Phase Day 18 • Moon Sign Sagittarius

am ....

pm ....

This would not be a good time to be forcing issues that will resolve themselves more successfully if you allow them space and time. On the other hand, who ever heard of a Gemini that could avoid 'tampering'? If you do feel obliged to interfere, make certain that you know what you are talking about.

11 SUNDAY

Moon Phase Day 19 • Moon Sign Sagittarius

am ....

pm ....

The actions of your partner can prove to be especially significant at this time and even younger members of the family are worth listening to if you are to get an all-round picture of the world as it stands at this moment in time. Interests outside of your own home and surroundings could have a fascination now.

NEGATIVE TREND						POSITIVE TREND				
-5	-4	-3	-2	-1		+1	+2	+3	+4	+5
					LOVE					
					MONEY					
					LUCK					
					VITALITY					

12 MONDAY   *Moon Phase Day 20 • Moon Sign Capricorn*

am ....

pm ....

Energy and vitality return in no uncertain terms. Be as honest with yourself as it is possible to be, particularly where possible changes in your working life are concerned. If you have new superiors remember that it is the nature of new brooms to sweep clean and that your natural charm should soon tone things down.

13 TUESDAY   *Moon Phase Day 21• Moon Sign Capricorn*

am ....

pm ....

Beware of a tendency to allow extravagance to get in your way. So far this year you have managed to avoid the excesses that such an attitude can bring and in any case you are not a lover of 'things' for their own sake, being far more of a thinker than most people would realise. Rest is easy to envisage but hard to find.

14 WEDNESDAY   *Moon Phase Day 22 • Moon Sign Capricorn*

am ....

pm ....

Capricorn news from far and wide is likely to be dropping on your mat at this point in time and could turn your mind towards foreign shores and sleepy lagoons. Not everyone can take themselves off at a whim, but if you are a person who can, now would be a really excellent time for even the shortest of outings.

15 THURSDAY   *Moon Phase Day 23 • Moon Sign Aquarius*

am ....

pm ....

It could seem counter-productive to stop and take stock when you are in the middle of a project. This is exactly what you are likely to be doing at the moment and if anything, the situation turns out better as a result. The hardest part is in persuading others that you know what you are doing and can be trusted.

16 FRIDAY
Moon Phase Day 24 • Moon Sign Aquarius

am ....

pm ....

Your sense of justice is especially well tuned at the present time, and not just on your own account either. It's likely that you will be doing all you can to stick up for the underdog now and you will need to be careful, despite your laudable actions, that you don't get more involved than might prove to be good for you.

17 SATURDAY
Moon Phase Day 25 • Moon Sign Pisces

am ....

pm ....

It's hard to shake off the feeling that people from outside your own immediate circle are interfering with your plans and making certain situations more difficult than they would otherwise be. Although you are being told that things are probably for your own good there is every chance that you will fail to recognise the fact.

18 SUNDAY
Moon Phase Day 26 • Moon Sign Pisces

am ....

pm ....

Better lines of communication now make it less difficult to appreciate that other people genuinely do believe that they are working on your behalf and that they want to be friends. The trouble is that you are still not in your normally accommodating mood and feel like being on your own more than people are used to.

← NEGATIVE TREND						POSITIVE TREND →				
-5	-4	-3	-2	-1		+1	+2	+3	+4	+5
					LOVE					
					MONEY					
					LUCK					
					VITALITY					

19 MONDAY   *Moon Phase Day 27 • Moon Sign Pisces*

am ....

pm ....

Your ambition and co-operative skills now begin to return,
probably making for an especially good time on the work front. It
ought to be possible to get enjoyment from the most mundane jobs
at the present time and you can also find spare moments to help
your friends come to terms with changes in their lives.

20 TUESDAY   *Moon Phase Day 28 • Moon Sign Aries*

am ....

pm ....

All the private matters in your life represent the areas that you are
turning to, at least as far as your mind is concerned. For a sign
that is always accused of being shallow, it's amazing just how
deeply your thoughts run. Trying to explain this fact to other
people would probably be a waste of time though.

21 WEDNESDAY   *Moon Phase Day 0 • Moon Sign Aries*

am ....

pm ....

Even though you feel in the mood to be in close touch with your
friends, there is a chance that your invitations will fall on stony
ground. Since you are more susceptible to paranoia than would
usually be the case it is important to realise that it is nothing to do
with you that makes your friends want stay at home.

22 THURSDAY   *Moon Phase Day 1 • Moon Sign Taurus*

am ....

pm ....

If you are still feeling socially isolated, perhaps you ought to take
stock of the position as it stands with regard to the people that you
generally mix with. In all probability they usually make the effort to come and see you and it might be good to jump in the car or
on the bus and return a visit or two yourself.

23 FRIDAY
Moon Phase Day 2 • Moon Sign Taurus

am ....

pm ....

Held back by practical matters, it isn't as simple as you would wish at the present time, to find the hours that you need to come to terms with the changing needs of your own life. Find the time at least to discuss common financial interests with your life-partner or the people that you mix with in a domestic sense.

24 SATURDAY
Moon Phase Day 3 • Moon Sign Gemini

am ....

pm ....

Turning your mind away from the restrictions that the working week has placed upon you, you are now in a far better position to be looking at the personal relationships that are so important to your life as a whole. Try to find some time to get out and about with the family, even if it is only to visit the shops.

25 SUNDAY
Moon Phase Day 4 • Moon Sign Gemini

am ....

pm ....

The Moon finds her way to your sign, in time for you to enjoy the benefits of the lunar high on a Sunday. The sky is truly the limit as far as you are concerned at this time, so if you don't enjoy yourself and bring happiness into the lives of other people at the same time, you really aren't trying.

← NEGATIVE TREND						POSITIVE TREND →				
-5	-4	-3	-2	-1		+1	+2	+3	+4	+5
					LOVE					
					MONEY					
					LUCK					
					VITALITY					

26 MONDAY   *Moon Phase Day 5 • Moon Sign Gemini*

am ....

pm ....

Things are speeding up rapidly and you should find yourself to be more dexterous than you have been for a long time. Take every opportunity to use this period for all that it is worth and encourage colleagues to have a go at things that they have avoided in the past. Your persuasive skills are strong.

27 TUESDAY   *Moon Phase Day 6 • Moon Sign Cancer*

am ....

pm ....

A boost to your finances seems likely now, probably as a result of efforts that you have put in long ago. If you are in a job that entails mixing with the general public, you can do your company some great favours now and should be on the receiving end of compliments, as a result of effort above and beyond the call of duty.

28 WEDNESDAY   *Moon Phase Day 7 • Moon Sign Cancer*

am ....

pm ....

A newsy and entertaining day allows you to side-step the mid-week blues that can often beset your reactive and quite unpredictable zodiac sign. One word of caution though. You are not a machine, and no matter how good you might be feeling, you do need to get some rest and relaxation at the end of the day.

29 THURSDAY   *Moon Phase Day 8 • Moon Sign Leo*

am ....

pm ....

Still generally on the move, you are in the middle of the kind of period that can lead to great happiness but also physical ruin for some Gemini people, especially the type that think they can burn the candle at both ends indefinitely. Trust a friend to speak the truth about a romantic matter that concerns you.

30 FRIDAY
Moon Phase Day 9 • Moon Sign Leo

am ....

pm ....

As the month ends, so does your run of luck, at least in terms of intensity. There are discussions taking place and you will have to think twice before you express an opinion. Whether it is an honest one or not will probably depend on what universe your mind happens to be in when you are asked to state your case.

1 SATURDAY
Moon Phase Day 10 • Moon Sign Virgo

am ....

pm ....

It would appear that a percentage of your thoughts are being directed towards affairs of the heart on this first of May. There is a tendency for you to be relying heavily upon other people in an emotional sense and to be sticking as much as you can to locations where security is easy to find.

2 SUNDAY
Moon Phase Day 11 • Moon Sign Virgo

am ....

pm ....

Where other people generally are concerned, and especially oversensitive relations, a softly softly approach needs to adopted. Direct approaches look as though they are going to offer a less positive response and one of the main problems about today is that you can't seem to get a sensible answer from anyone at all.

← NEGATIVE TREND							POSITIVE TREND →				
-5	-4	-3	-2	-1			+1	+2	+3	+4	+5
					LOVE						
					MONEY						
					LUCK						
					VITALITY						

1993

YOUR MONTH AT A GLANCE

The twelve numbered boxes represent the important areas in your life.
The key to the numbers you will find beneath the panel. A Sun above
the number indicates that opportunities are around. A Cloud below
the number, that you should be a bit defensive. Nothing above or
below and life will be pretty ordinary.

☀			☀				☀				
1	2	3	4	5	6	7	8	9	10	11	12

KEY

1 Strength of Personality
2 Personal Finance
3 Useful Information Gathering
4 Domestic Affairs
5 Pleasure & Romance
6 Effective Work & Health
7 One to One Relationships
8 Questioning, Thinking & Deciding
9 External Influences / Education
10 Career Aspirations
11 Teamwork Activities
12 Unconscious Impulses

MAY HIGHS AND LOWS

Here, I show how the rhythm of the Moon will affect you this month.
Like the tide, your energies and abilities will rise and fall with its pattern. When it is above the date line, go-for-it. When it is below the
line you should be resting.

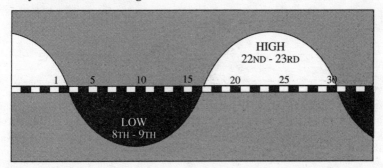

3 MONDAY
Moon Phase Day 12 • Moon Sign Virgo

am ....

pm ....

The actions of the people around you are still a little odd, though are now more likely to bring a smile to your face than a look of frustration. This is not a favourable time to be thinking about gambling, either with cash or with the emotions of other people, so be certain to tread carefully if you can.

4 TUESDAY
Moon Phase Day 13 • Moon Sign Libra

am ....

pm ....

Now much more inclined to be really listening to what the people that you work and mix with socially are saying than would usually be the case, you might be more than a little surprised by some of the home truths that come to light. Of course listening carefully also means being more willing to help out too!

5 WEDNESDAY
Moon Phase Day 14 • Moon Sign Libra

am ....

pm ....

It's heavy going at work for some children of Mercury at the moment and if you are one of them, part of the fault might be that, contrary to your usual nature, you have a tendency to take yourself too seriously just now. If this extends to the tasks you are undertaking as well, no wonder you are out of sorts.

6 THURSDAY
Moon Phase Day 15 • Moon Sign Scorpio

am ....

pm ....

Where it is possible, you would probably choose to work on your own now, or at least with people that you know you are likely to get on with extremely well. You can be quite touchy, though half the battle is being able to recognise the fact and compensating for what is after all a very temporary phenomena.

7 FRIDAY
Moon Phase Day 16 • Moon Sign Scorpio

am ....

pm ....

It has to be said that there have been one or two hiccups in your life
at the start of the month, though recognising them is half the battle.
Life should be settling down somewhat now, and that much quicker
if you don't dwell on things that you have no control over in any
case. All the same, try to avoid being a passive observer.

8 SATURDAY
Moon Phase Day 17 • Moon Sign Sagittarius

am ....

pm ....

Now that the lunar low is upon you, it is very likely that you are
going to find the weekend to be a generally quiet one, and since
there is no point in swimming against the tide too much at this point
in time, why not enjoy what life dishes out. Social hours spent with
friends can prove to be especially rewarding.

9 SUNDAY
Moon Phase Day 18 • Moon Sign Sagittarius

am ....

pm ....

There is no doubt that dealing with rather difficult people has been
something that you have had to take in your stride recently, and as
far as family members are concerned this pattern could still be holding true. All the more reason to stick to close friends in your free
hours for the present because they will make fewer demands of you.

← *NEGATIVE TREND*   *POSITIVE TREND* →

-5	-4	-3	-2	-1		+1	+2	+3	+4	+5
					LOVE					
					MONEY					
					LUCK					
					VITALITY					

10 MONDAY
Moon Phase Day 19 • Moon Sign Capricorn

am ....

pm ....

Circumstances conspire to encourage the softer and more sensitive Gemini to put in an appearance as the working week opens. Career-wise there is some 'one-upmanship' about, though it is probably best not to become involved if you have any choice in the matter at all. Be careful in all your financial transactions.

11 TUESDAY
Moon Phase Day 20 • Moon Sign Capricorn

am ....

pm ....

The adage that 'a change is as good as a rest' has never been more true than in your life now. Let's face it, if there is one sign of the zodiac that is going to become bored with routines all too easily, it is yours. You might not be able to alter your working hours all that much, though you can certainly ring the changes later.

12 WEDNESDAY
Moon Phase Day 21 • Moon Sign Aquarius

am ....

pm ....

Niggles can lead to a level of anxiety far beyond the expected norm and a tendency towards worry that may even surprise you. It might be a good thing to make a point of listening to the worries of a friend later in the day. Not only will you be doing them a favour but it should help to get your own situations into perspective.

13 THURSDAY
Moon Phase Day 22 • Moon Sign Aquarius

am ....

pm ....

Power to influence your own life is now starting to return, though that doesn't mean to say that you will choose to exercise it under all circumstances. For example, you have a chance to even the score where an old disagreement is concerned, but is the situation one that still seems important enough for you to bother with?

110

YOUR DAILY GUIDE TO MAY 1993

14 FRIDAY
Moon Phase Day 23 • Moon Sign Aquarius

am ....

pm ....

Career prospects should now be taking a turn for the better and good news also seems to be coming in from a number of different directions. The areas of life that take your fancy at the moment probably include your social sphere, which may have been slightly dull of late. Avoid analysis and think about instinctive reaction.

15 SATURDAY
Moon Phase Day 24 • Moon Sign Pisces

am ....

pm ....

No matter how much the obstacles of the first half of the month still seem to press in on you from time to time, there can be no turning back, certainly as far as this weekend is concerned. Many of the niggles that still manifest themselves have far more to do with the way that your mind is working, so constructive thinking is vital.

16 SUNDAY
Moon Phase Day 25 • Moon Sign Pisces

am ....

pm ....

With a strong show of loyalty from friends and masses of love from your closest relatives, it ought to be easy to leave the practical world behind and think about the social implications of what could be a really happy day. Any obstacles that do occur can be dealt with one at a time. This is not a good period for 'block worries'.

← *NEGATIVE TREND*   *POSITIVE TREND* →

-5	-4	-3	-2	-1			+1	+2	+3	+4	+5
					LOVE						
					MONEY						
					LUCK						
					VITALITY						

17 MONDAY
Moon Phase Day 26 • Moon Sign Aries

am ....

pm ....

Much of the success inherent in this working week depends on the degree of relaxation that you are able to inject into even the most routine of tasks. It is best for Gemini people to take stock occasionally, not of what you are doing, but of the attitude that you have on the way.

18 TUESDAY
Moon Phase Day 27 • Moon Sign Aries

am ....

pm ....

Mercury is in your first solar house now and there are many comings and goings to brighten up your life no end. As is often the case you are full of good ideas and may lack only the cash and the time to put them into action. Time becomes more flexible from now on and money turns out to be far less of the problem.

19 WEDNESDAY
Moon Phase Day 28 • Moon Sign Aries

am ....

pm ....

The various pressures of a busy and demanding world are not always appealing, even to you; which is why you might decide that the time is right for a break of some sort. A change of scenery would do you the world of good, though if this is not possible an excursion in your mind, possibly by way of a good book, might be equally useful.

20 THURSDAY
Moon Phase Day 29 • Moon Sign Taurus

am ....

pm ....

That old Gemini demon, boredom, could quite easily be paying you a short but noticeable visit now, and you have to get your thinking cap on if you are going to avoid its influences. In reality, all you have to do is to take a look around, and don't allow yourself to be dragged down by people who tend to be depressive types by nature.

21 FRIDAY   *Moon Phase Day 0 • Moon Sign Taurus*

am ....

pm ....

The Sun now enters the first house of your solar chart, a fortunate situation as far as your general life is concerned. You are likely to discover over the next three or four weeks that you achieve a greater degree of satisfaction from even your most routine efforts and that other people are willing to put themselves out on your behalf.

22 SATURDAY   *Moon Phase Day 1 • Moon Sign Gemini*

am ....

pm ....

You are now embarking on what could easily turn out to be the best two days that you are going to experience this month. With the lunar high now on your side you have plenty of energy and the ability to push many of your plans through easily and without any undue fuss. Family matters seem less constricting.

23 SUNDAY   *Moon Phase Day 2 • Moon Sign Gemini*

am ....

pm ....

Even everyday events take on a new meaning and there is a clarity to everything that you do that proves to be infectious as far as your friends are concerned too. This helps to put you centre-stage in a social sense and means that the sky is the limit as far as the sort of invitations that you receive are concerned.

← *NEGATIVE TREND*   *POSITIVE TREND* →

-5	-4	-3	-2	-1		+1	+2	+3	+4	+5
					LOVE					
					MONEY					
					LUCK					
					VITALITY					

24 MONDAY

Moon Phase Day 3 • Moon Sign Cancer

am ....

pm ....

Saturn now enters your solar tenth house and helps to change things for the better even more. Any turbulence in career matters is now calming down and your clarity of vision appears to know no bounds. Tangible rewards in a financial sense are yours for the taking at the present time, even if you have to wait a while.

25 TUESDAY

Moon Phase Day 4 • Moon Sign Cancer

am ....

pm ....

With your health and vitality boosted, you don't have to work especially hard to win the approval of other people for ideas and projects that you personally know to be very sound. Your persuasive skills have seldom been better, though you do have a tendency to overlook important details in your anxiety to get things done.

26 WEDNESDAY

Moon Phase Day 5 • Moon Sign Cancer

am ....

pm ....

Certain aspects would seem to indicate that you may have been somewhat reticent to take others into your confidence recently, especially as far as romantic issues are concerned. Now you are far less secretive and willing to talk to almost anyone who wants to listen. Choose your confidant with care.

27 THURSDAY

Moon Phase Day 6 • Moon Sign Leo

am ....

pm ....

Others are almost certain to envy your poise and natural talents just now, even though they can't see the indecision that is at work inside you for much of the time. This is a period when your personal and romantic prospects are especially good and when you seek as much variety in your life as is humanly possible.

28 FRIDAY   *Moon Phase Day 7 • Moon Sign Leo*

am ....

pm ....

As the working week draws to a close it is very important to make certain that you have your priorities right and that you are not making too much out of situations that would put themselves right if you were only willing to give them time. Authority figures seem to be throwing their weight about a little.

29 SATURDAY   *Moon Phase Day 8 • Moon Sign Virgo*

am ....

pm ....

Family matters need looking at closely, so the weekend could not have come at a better time for you. Spend some time with your loved ones if you can and make certain that you tackle jobs around the house carefully and only one at a time. Many social gatherings and friendly meetings can be expected round about now.

30 SUNDAY   *Moon Phase Day 9 • Moon Sign Virgo*

am ....

pm ....

You want to have fun and definitely are not now in the mood for taking anything especially seriously. It isn't certain that the people you mix with are going to be as 'free' in their attitudes as you are, so if all else fails, allow a certain period of time to listen to what they have to say before you carry on with the enjoyment.

← NEGATIVE TREND								POSITIVE TREND →		
-5	-4	-3	-2	-1			+1	+2	+3	+4	+5

					LOVE					
					MONEY					
					LUCK					
					VITALITY					

31 MONDAY   *Moon Phase Day 10 • Moon Sign Libra*

am ....

pm ....

The emphasis as May ends is on co-operative ventures of all kinds, especially those that may have a bearing on your working life. In love there is liable to be an especially high point, though possibly some restlessness too if you can't make your partner understand exactly why you think about some situations in the way that you do.

1 TUESDAY   *Moon Phase Day 11 • Moon Sign Libra*

am ....

pm ....

Partly because the Sun now occupies your own sign of Gemini, and also because you are so optimistic, you should now find that many of your most cherished ambitions have a chance of turning out as you had hoped. The everyday facts of life may not hold a lot of excitement but socially at least new projects do abound.

2 WEDNESDAY   *Moon Phase Day 12 • Moon Sign Scorpio*

am ....

pm ....

Mercury speeds into your solar second house and the bright and breezy attitude that so typifies your zodiac sign is on show almost twenty-four hours of the day. It isn't hard to take on a more taxing role professionally because you have so much energy at the present time, though perhaps you should give some thought to later!

3 THURSDAY   *Moor Phase Day 13 • Moon Sign Scorpio*

am ....

pm ....

Now that the lunar low is about to begin pressing in on you, jobs that seemed so easy only a day or two ago can appear to be quite intimidating by comparison. Make more provision for short periods of rest and recuperation than you have been willing to do of late and be certain to plan now for the social possibilities of the weekend.

116

4 FRIDAY   *Moon Phase Day 14 • Moon Sign Sagittarius*

am ....

pm ....

The arrival of the lunar low is bound to mean less available energy
and can also slow you down in a workaday sense. Your lightning
quick thought processes are also less speedy than you would normally expect, though you wouldn't work your legs until you collapsed so
what makes your mind any different?

5 SATURDAY   *Moon Phase Day 15 • Moon Sign Sagittarius*

am ....

pm ....

Matters that have been hidden for a while now begin to come to
light, probably because circumstances have given you more time to
look at things in greater detail and freed from the fetters of practical day to day concerns. Aches and pains should be listened to,
there are important messages about posture and usage.

6 SUNDAY   *Moon Phase Day 16 • Moon Sign Capricorn*

am ....

pm ....

While you haven't particularly been looking, there is a chance that
your popularity has improved of its own accord. If you have any
delicate domestic or personal situations to sort out, it would be a
very good idea to make certain that you are fully in command of the
situation before you go in with all guns blazing.

← NEGATIVE TREND						*POSITIVE TREND →*				
-5	-4	-3	-2	-1		+1	+2	+3	+4	+5
					LOVE					
					MONEY					
					LUCK					
					VITALITY					

1993

YOUR MONTH AT A GLANCE

The twelve numbered boxes represent the important areas in your life. The key to the numbers you will find beneath the panel. A Sun above the number indicates that opportunities are around. A Cloud below the number, that you should be a bit defensive. Nothing above or below and life will be pretty ordinary.

1	2	3	4	5	6	7	8	9	10	11	12

KEY

1 Strength of Personality
2 Personal Finance
3 Useful Information Gathering
4 Domestic Affairs
5 Pleasure & Romance
6 Effective Work & Health

7 One to One Relationships
8 Questioning, Thinking & Deciding
9 External Influences / Education
10 Career Aspirations
11 Teamwork Activities
12 Unconscious Impulses

JUNE HIGHS AND LOWS

Here, I show how the rhythm of the Moon will affect you this month. Like the tide, your energies and abilities will rise and fall with its pattern. When it is above the date line, go-for-it. When it is below the line you should be resting.

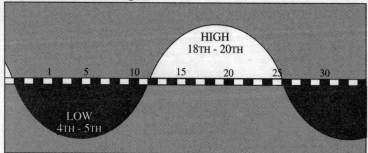

HIGH
18TH - 20TH

LOW
4TH - 5TH

118

7 MONDAY
Moon Phase Day 17 • Moon Sign Capricorn

am ....

pm ....

Venus is now in your solar twelfth house and although certain aspects of your personal life are less exciting than they might have been recently, there is also a chance that they could be less stressed too. Favourable practical issues originate at this time and you may soon have more control over the practical considerations of life.

8 TUESDAY
Moon Phase Day 18 • Moon Sign Capricorn

am ....

pm ....

Although it is very important to follow tried and tested paths in the main, that doesn't mean that you should forget more adventurous plans altogether. At home there are situations that will need handling with kid gloves, probably associated with younger or older people and certainly tied to family relationships in some way.

9 WEDNESDAY
Moon Phase Day 19 • Moon Sign Aquarius

am ....

pm ....

You cannot fail to notice the need that you now have for a greater degree of social change and for travel too. Staying in one place and doing the same old things is certain to get you down at the present time and all chances to break the fetters of conventional living will be taken for what they are worth.

10 THURSDAY
Moon Phase Day 20 • Moon Sign Aquarius

am ....

pm ....

Suddenly busy trying to balance the needs of several different spheres of your life, all at the same time. your restlessness can become even more acute. Outside of actually having things to do, it's important to allow your mind to wander and also to chat to interesting people whenever the possibility arises.

119

11 FRIDAY
Moon Phase Day 21 • Moon Sign Pisces

am ....

pm ....

Look out for a greater degree of personal satisfaction now and for more control over the way that especially tricky situations appear to be finding their own solutions. In disputes that don't involve you directly it will be important to see both sides of the argument but still not become personally involved.

12 SATURDAY
Moon Phase Day 22 • Moon Sign Pisces

am ....

pm...

Some people in your vicinity are in for a rude awakening, though you are likely to resist the temptation to say 'I told you so!' On the contrary it is more likely that you will offer what assistance you can and hope that the person concerned will rely on you more in the future. Some difficulties in your love life need addressing.

13 SUNDAY
Moon Phase Day 23 • Moon Sign Aries

am ....

pm...

A better spirit of teamwork is now available in a domestic sense, allowing jobs to get done in half the time and also creating a more favourable atmosphere is which to discuss the possibility of far reaching changes that could have a bearing on everyone that you live with. Listen to all points of view.

← NEGATIVE TREND						POSITIVE TREND →				
-5	-4	-3	-2	-1		+1	+2	+3	+4	+5
					LOVE					
					MONEY					
					LUCK					
					VITALITY					

14 MONDAY   *Moon Phase Day 24 • Moon Sign Aries*

am ....

pm ....

Beware of people who appear to say one thing and yet are inclined to
be doing another. If there is one time in the month when you are
likely to be duped, that period is now. It isn't that you lack common
sense, though you can be far too trusting at the moment and inclined
to take everything at face value.

15 TUESDAY   *Moon Phase Day 25 • Moon Sign Aries*

am ....

pm ....

Taking one step backward for every two that you go forward, you
might be forgiven for believing that life is something of a struggle at
the present time. Nevertheless, you are making far more progress
than you could possibly realise and will be on the receiving end of
very positive happenings quite soon.

16 WEDNESDAY   *Moon Phase Day 26 • Moon Sign Taurus*

am ....

pm ....

Relaxed and comfortable at the present time, you will still be
anxious to be inhabiting your own space and probably won't want to
be moving around any more than circumstances necessitate. It is
still important to talk to others and to let them know how you are
feeling and the aspects of life that are important to you.

17 THURSDAY   *Moon Phase Day 27 • Moon Sign Taurus*

am ....

pm ....

Good news is likely to be coming in regarding some of your most important ambitions but don't allow yourself to become over oppor-
tunistic. Some help from colleagues and friends is to be expected;
the sort of assistance that turns out to be very practical and points
you in some surprising directions.

18 FRIDAY

Moon Phase Day 28 • Moon Sign Gemini

am ....

pm ....

The lunar high is likely to put you in a good mood, as well as supplying you with enough energy to do what you you feel is important in a personal sense. There is a tendency to take personal risks that might not be too advisable at the present time but there won't be anyone around who is brave enough to tell you.

19 SATURDAY

Moon Phase Day 29 • Moon Sign Gemini

am ....

pm ....

Your impact on the world in general is especially good now and social mixing probably turns out to be the most important aspect of the weekend. In your personal life it is possible to get your own way, despite the fact that you find yourself in the company of people who are almost as determined as you are right now.

20 SUNDAY

Moon Phase Day 0 • Moon Sign Gemini

am ....

pm ....

Others are inclined to push you forward, assuming that you always want to be in the limelight. Fortunately, at the present time they are right, though there is a side to your nature that is inclined to seek out solitude, which is more likely to show itself on occasions during the week ahead. In the meantime, you are a star.

← NEGATIVE TREND						POSITIVE TREND →				
-5	-4	-3	-2	-1		+1	+2	+3	+4	+5
					LOVE					
					MONEY					
					LUCK					
					VITALITY					

21 MONDAY
Moon Phase Day 1 • Moon Sign Cancer

am ....

pm ....

With the Sun moving into your solar second house, there is more of a tendency for the extravagant side of your nature to be on display, making you penny-wise but pound-foolish. Despite this, it is possible to make some important acquisitions, because some of them have nothing to do with your financial state at all.

22 TUESDAY
Moon Phase Day 2 • Moon Sign Cancer

am ....

pm ....

Prepare yourself for a flurry of activity and for a need of constant reassurance. This is a time of contradictions, and it is now that a more pensive quality begins to be the most noticeable aspect of your nature. Don't worry about the sudden role reversal, it's part of the reason that people warm to you so much.

23 WEDNESDAY
Moon Phase Day 3 • Moon Sign Leo

am ....

pm ....

With Mars now in your solar fourth house, the energy of this high-powered planet is evident in a domestic and home based sense. The people that you live with are full of energy and inclined to make you dizzy with their coming and going. For your part, you need to find a quiet corner and think.

24 THURSDAY
Moon Phase Day 4 • Moon Sign Leo

am ....

pm ....

Always ready to have a look at the unusual, you are inclined to be as constant in your moods as the weather, which is why you are quite happy be dumping responsibility and doing whatever takes your fancy. Chances are that you have done your thinking and so it's action all the way.

25 FRIDAY

Moon Phase Day 5 • Moon Sign Virgo

am ....

pm ....

How do you get away with it? A bright and happy atmosphere is
your lot, and mainly of your creation. Domestic issues lighten your
load and the people that you are mixing with also help to make for
an interesting end of the week interlude. It's business as usual in a
professional sense and you will want to be tying up some loose ends.

26 SATURDAY

Moon Phase Day 6 • Moon Sign Virgo

am ....

pm ....

There is more time for intimate relationships now and for getting to
know how your closest relatives feel about things. It might not be
possible to do everything that appeals to you at the moment, and
you do need at least some time for a change of scenery, even if it is
only going to the shops.

27 SUNDAY

Moon Phase Day 7 • Moon Sign Libra

am ....

pm ....

A time to catch up on some fun and to be doing the things that appeal to you at the time. There are plenty of responsibilities coming
up next week, and you will cope with them much better if you main-
tain a happy-go-lucky attitude to life now. In all situations it is the
'fun' side of life that takes your fancy.

← NEGATIVE TREND						POSITIVE TREND →				
-5	-4	-3	-2	-1		+1	+2	+3	+4	+5
					LOVE					
					MONEY					
					LUCK					
					VITALITY					

28 MONDAY   *Moon Phase Day 8 • Moon Sign Libra*

am ....

pm ....

Colleagues are going to be in a difficult frame of mind, and it's lucky that you are feeling so diplomatic and easy-going yourself. Petty disagreements, especially regarding finances, are beneath your dignity at the present time, nor will you want to become involved in the romantic disputes of your friends.

29 TUESDAY   *Moon Phase Day 9 • Moon Sign Scorpio*

am ....

pm ....

Because you are so wrapped up in practical matters, you could be missing some of the most important aspects of this extremely busy day. Conversation tends to be quite superficial and inclines you to wonder what the people that you mix with are really thinking about. For your part, please yourself.

30 WEDNESDAY   *Moon Phase Day 10 • Moon Sign Scorpio*

am ....

pm ....

There are some especially tricky issues around and as a result you finish the month in a somewhat puzzled mood. Easy solutions to business problems may not be the ones that you should opt for. Better to do nothing for a day or two than to take actions now that you could well feel annoyed about later.

1 THURSDAY   *Moon Phase Day 11 • Moon Sign Sagittarius*

am ....

pm ....

Commencing July with the lunar low may not appear to give you the incentive that you really need to get off to a flying start. On the other hand you have been through a fairly hectic period in the recent past and might well gain in the long-term from a short, enforced period of relaxation at the moment.

2 FRIDAY
Moon Phase Day 12 • Moon Sign Sagittarius

am ....

pm ....

Things are probably still too quiet for your liking, and many Geminis such as yourself will be champing at the bit in a desire to push things along more quickly. Remember though, this is the part of the monthly lunar cycle when aspects of your nature are regenerating, and there is at least more time for self-indulgence.

3 SATURDAY
Moon Phase Day 13 • Moon Sign Sagittarius

am ....

pm ....

Any career pressures that have beset you of late should now begin to diminish. Life generally begins to speed up noticeably, and though you may be on the receiving end as far as one or two knocks in a practical sense are concerned, this should mark the commencement of a more active period to come.

4 SUNDAY
Moon Phase Day 14 • Moon Sign Capricorn

am ....

pm ....

Practical issues hang in the balance. Even so your intuitive feelings are strong and can act as the most positive guide as to how you should be behaving. The area of your life that is almost certain to bring the greatest pleasure at the present time involves personal relationships and the way you are reacting to them.

← NEGATIVE TREND							POSITIVE TREND →			
-5	-4	-3	-2	-1		+1	+2	+3	+4	+5
					LOVE					
					MONEY					
					LUCK					
					VITALITY					

1993

YOUR MONTH AT A GLANCE

The twelve numbered boxes represent the important areas in your life.
The key to the numbers you will find beneath the panel. A Sun above
the number indicates that opportunities are around. A Cloud below
the number, that you should be a bit defensive. Nothing above or
below and life will be pretty ordinary.

		☀				☀					☀
1	2	3	4	5	6	7	8	9	10	11	12
					☁			☁			

KEY	
1 Strength of Personality	7 One to One Relationships
2 Personal Finance	8 Questioning, Thinking & Deciding
3 Useful Information Gathering	9 External Influences / Education
4 Domestic Affairs	10 Career Aspirations
5 Pleasure & Romance	11 Teamwork Activities
6 Effective Work & Health	12 Unconscious Impulses

JULY HIGHS AND LOWS

Here, I show how the rhythm of the Moon will affect you this month.
Like the tide, your energies and abilities will rise and fall with its pattern. When it is above the date line, go-for-it. When it is below the
line you should be resting.

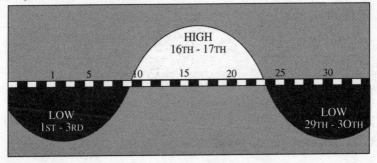

5 MONDAY
Moon Phase Day 15 • Moon Sign Capricorn

am ....

pm...

Leave no stone unturned in your efforts to make your lot easier in a
practical and professional sense. A mixture of careful analysis and
intuitive insight works best and, rather than making the same mistakes all over again, this would be a good day to cut your losses and
opt for completely new values.

6 TUESDAY
Moon Phase Day 16 • Moon Sign Aquarius

am ....

pm...

Venus, the planet of love, now makes an appearance in your own
sign of Gemini, giving a boost to your love life and enlarging your
popularity no end. Despite the fact that Venus in this position can
be very beneficial, it may also bestow upon you a tendency to be
more compromising than is really good for you.

7 WEDNESDAY
Moon Phase Day 17 • Moon Sign Aquarius

am ....

pm ....

Routine jobs are a chore, particularly those associated with aspects
of your social life that are fairly tedious in themselves. The people
that you come across generally are inclined to take themselves too
seriously, something that you rarely do and find difficult to cope
with in others.

8 THURSDAY
Moon Phase Day 18 • Moon Sign Pisces

am ....

pm ....

Assistance comes from the least likely directions now if you are willing to keep your eyes open and accept the help when it is on offer.
Although you could be annoyed at the fact that some of your instructions are being countermanded in a workaday sense, outside of your
profession, people are only too willing to listen.

9 FRIDAY
Moon Phase Day 19 • Moon Sign Pisces

am ....

pm ....
As far as finances go you could now find yourself in a stronger position than has been the case since the start of the month. All the same this isn't a time of immediate gratification and so there is liable to be a delay before you get your hands on any cash that does turn up. Friends turn out to be particularly wise.

10 SATURDAY
Moon Phase Day 20 • Moon Sign Pisces

am ....

pm ....
Love issues and pleasurable pursuits of all kinds can make this a weekend to remember for many of you. In order to get the best out of the period though, it is necessary for you to put a significant amount of effort in on your own behalf because the world is only going to sing your praises now if you do so first.

11 SUNDAY
Moon Phase Day 21 • Moon Sign Aries

am ....

pm ....
You have some very positive expectations, both of others and of life in general. There are occasions however when you are inclined to be too optimistic for your own good, and it appears likely that this is one of them. A practical view of life is out and the intuitive qualities that you enjoy are to the fore again.

← *NEGATIVE TREND* | *POSITIVE TREND* →

-5	-4	-3	-2	-1		+1	+2	+3	+4	+5
					LOVE					
					MONEY					
					LUCK					
					VITALITY					

12 MONDAY
Moon Phase Day 22 • Moon Sign Aries

am ....

pm..

There is a possibility that you might have the wool pulled over your eyes in a financial sense because not everyone that you come across at the moment will be as honest as they appear to be. Surprise encounters can have far reaching and very positive implications and a more stimulating social time is on the way.

13 TUESDAY
Moon Phase Day 23 • Moon Sign Taurus

am ....

pm..

At least it appears that you are now likely to be on the receiving end of the kind of credit that you deserve for the effort that you put into life, and especially into making other people happy. Now in a generally happy-go-lucky frame of mind, you appear to be taking no notice but in reality won't miss a trick.

14 WEDNESDAY
Moon Phase Day 24 • Moon Sign Taurus

am ....

pm ....

The possibilities that stand around you in a practical sense now are likely to be self-evident, so much the better because you don't have the time to play the detective when life carries so many exciting possibilities. Your personal life is jogging along in a fairly satisfactory way, though you might be chasing excitement.

15 THURSDAY
Moon Phase Day 25 • Moon Sign Taurus

am ....

pm ....

With the approach of the lunar high and the energy surge that it is likely to bring you, it wouldn't be a bad idea to have a rest today, if you can convince yourself to do so. There seems to be more things to do than there are hours to complete and perhaps you should slow yourself to a walking pace so that there is at least time to breath.

16 FRIDAY
Moon Phase Day 26 • Moon Sign Gemini

am ....

pm ....

You are very candid in your appraisal of most situations, which is probably more than can be said of many of the people that you are mixing with today. The lunar low shows just how much you can get through if you are willing to give yourself to the job in hand and practical help should be easy to come by.

17 SATURDAY
Moon Phase Day 27 • Moon Sign Gemini

am ....

pm ....

Decision making regarding personal matters can be a little tricky at times, mainly because you don't have your usual persuasive powers and are finding it difficult to bring others round to your point of view. The lunar low sees you pushing ahead in most things and indicates the use of certain strengths that you didn't know you had!

18 SUNDAY
Moon Phase Day 28 • Moon Sign Cancer

am ....

pm ....

There could be a rather 'routine' feel about this summer Sunday, and if so, you may only have yourself to blame. There is no reason at all for sticking to those things that you think are expected of you, even if you are correct in your assumptions. What you need is a touch of variety in your life.

← *NEGATIVE TREND*   *POSITIVE TREND* →

-5	-4	-3	-2	-1		+1	+2	+3	+4	+5
					LOVE					
					MONEY					
					LUCK					
					VITALITY					

131

19 MONDAY

Moon Phase Day 0 • Moon Sign Cancer

am ....

pm...

The way that some people are behaving is apt to indicate that there may be more than meets the eye concerning them than you have really considered before. Some close scrutiny of your financial situation is to be recommended, as long as you don't use the exercise as an excuse to worry about situations that you cannot control.

20 TUESDAY

Moon Phase Day 1 • Moon Sign Leo

am ....

pm...

If ever there was a time to sit back and blend into the scenery, that time for you is right now. Most people should recognise that you are in a very pensive mood and will leave you alone for once, though this may not be the case as far as colleagues are concerned and it is fair to say that work could be a problem.

21 WEDNESDAY

Moon Phase Day 2 • Moon Sign Leo

am ....

pm ....

There is a possibility that you are becoming a little too outspoken for your own good, a tendency that is not helped by the rather tense aspect between Mercury and Neptune in your solar chart at present. In addition, it becomes obvious to you that situations in a personal sense are not at all what they appear to be.

22 THURSDAY

Moon Phase Day 3 • Moon Sign Virgo

am ....

pm ....

There is a constant level of activity to come to terms with as far as your working life is concerned, and this is unlikely to afford you the time or energy that you need to make things the way that you would wish them to be at home or in a more personal area of your life. Patience is a virtue that you don't enjoy in abundance.

23 FRIDAY   *Moon Phase Day 4 • Moon Sign Virgo*

am ....

pm ....

With the Sun now entering the third house of your solar chart, although there is no slackening of the rather hectic pace that you insist on setting yourself, you should at least notice that you have an improved ability to express your feelings to the people who are most important in your life.

24 SATURDAY   *Moon Phase Day 5 • Moon Sign Libra*

am ....

pm ....

The show of affection that is coming in, both from relatives and from your dearest friends, looks like making this a weekend to remember. All considerations of actually getting anything constructive done will probably be out of the window, in favour of waiting to see what crops up of its own accord.

25 SUNDAY   *Moon Phase Day 6 • Moon Sign Libra*

am ....

pm ....

Sort term disappointments simply have to be accepted as a natural part of the way that your life is going right now, and have little tangible effect, as long as you realise that they will not hold you back in the longer term. Disputes at home are unlikely to be created by you, so don't get involved if you can help it.

| ← NEGATIVE TREND | | | | | | POSITIVE TREND → | | | | |
-5	-4	-3	-2	-1		+1	+2	+3	+4	+5
				■	LOVE					
					MONEY	■	■			
					LUCK	■				
					VITALITY	■				

133

26 MONDAY
Moon Phase Day 7 • Moon Sign Scorpio

am ....

pm...

Solid, practical progress is the order of the day and you may well even surprise yourself with the amount that you are able to get done, both at work and in a more personal sense. You have an in-built quality control concerning your love life and will want the very best for your partner, as well as for yourself.

27 TUESDAY
Moon Phase Day 8 • Moon Sign Scorpio

am ....

pm...

Although there are many people around you at the moment who would be only too willing to offer you all sorts of advice, in the end you will want to please yourself about what you do. This is especially true in a personal sense, an area of your life in which you will stand no interference of any sort.

28 WEDNESDAY
Moon Phase Day 9 • Moon Sign Scorpio

am ....

pm ....

The advancing Moon now reaches a position that places it almost opposite to your own sign of Gemini, and as always with the lunar low, that means that vitality is not what you would want it to be. The situation is not aided by this being the middle of the week, hardly your favourite time. Watch and listen - don't act.

29 THURSDAY
Moon Phase Day 10 • Moon Sign Sagittarius

am ....

pm ....

Don't try to force practical matters to come to a head now and if it is at all possible, consider yourself to be a spectator in the game of life, rather than a participant for the next couple of days. Friends are helpful and warm, only too willing to put themselves out for you, and the feeling is mutual.

30 FRIDAY
Moon Phase Day 11 • Moon Sign Sagittarius

am ....

pm ....

The actions of your partner can be very telling at the moment, showing a high level of concern in practically everything that they do. Those Geminis who have been thinking about some sort of health regime could well be looking towards this period to commence. The best advice would be to wait a while.

31 SATURDAY
Moon Phase Day 12 • Moon Sign Capricorn

am ....

pm ....

Delays in a fiscal sense are more or less inevitable as the month finishes on what appears to be a somewhat negative note. It is very important to bear the sensitivity of other people in mind as the weekend unfolds, though not if to do so means shifting your world a thousand miles from its allotted course

1 SUNDAY
Moon Phase Day 13 • Moon Sign Capricorn

am ....

pm ....

It would seem that the change of the month has a very tangible effect on how you are thinking, and by implication on the way that your life is starting to unfold. Romantic and generally personal situations are now more jolly and allow greater freedom than would have been possible last week.

← *NEGATIVE TREND*   *POSITIVE TREND* →

-5	-4	-3	-2	-1		+1	+2	+3	+4	+5
					LOVE					
					MONEY					
					LUCK					
					VITALITY					

AUGUST
1993

YOUR MONTH AT A GLANCE

The twelve numbered boxes represent the important areas in your life. The key to the numbers you will find beneath the panel. A Sun above the number indicates that opportunities are around. A Cloud below the number, that you should be a bit defensive. Nothing above or below and life will be pretty ordinary.

1	2	3	4	5	6	7	8	9	10	11	12

KEY

1 Strength of Personality
2 Personal Finance
3 Useful Information Gathering
4 Domestic Affairs
5 Pleasure & Romance
6 Effective Work & Health

7 One to One Relationships
8 Questioning, Thinking & Deciding
9 External Influences / Education
10 Career Aspirations
11 Teamwork Activities
12 Unconscious Impulses

AUGUST HIGHS AND LOWS

Here, I show how the rhythm of the Moon will affect you this month. Like the tide, your energies and abilities will rise and fall with its pattern. When it is above the date line, go-for-it. When it is below the line you should be resting.

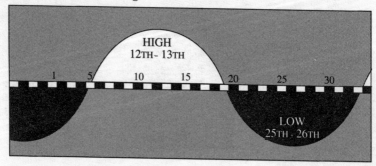

HIGH
12TH - 13TH

LOW
25TH - 26TH

2 MONDAY   *Moon Phase Day 14 • Moon Sign Aquarius*

am ....

pm ....

Thoughts revolving around the commencement of exciting changes, probably associated with travel, make the start of the working week very much more exciting than you might have expected it to be. It will take a 'carrot and stick' approach to make other people toe the line, or a strong dose of your verbal common sense.

3 TUESDAY   *Moon Phase Day 15 • Moon Sign Aquarius*

am ....

pm ....

With Venus now in your solar second house, you should find it less difficult to attend to the 'good things of life' and will once more be turning your mind towards thoughts of travel and exploration. All relationships, even casual ones, turn out to be very supportive and tedious jobs take on a new and more exciting aspect.

4 WEDNESDAY   *Moon Phase Day 16 • Moon Sign Aquarius*

am ....

pm ....

The pressure is now on in a career sense for many children of Mercury, not that you notice the fact particularly at a time when you are recognising tasks and getting on with them as quickly and efficiently as you can. Job descriptions that indicate 'needs to work hard and with sound initiative' could have been written for you.

5 THURSDAY   *Moon Phase Day 17 • Moon Sign Pisces*

am ....

pm ....

Emotional pressures now begin to melt into the scenery, and there is little or nothing to prevent you from achieving the kind of understanding with relatives that has been lacking in your life for a little while. Delays in putting personal health routines into practice are ended and success is more or less assured.

6 FRIDAY
Moon Phase Day 18 • Moon Sign Pisces

am ....

pm ....

Because you are in such a determined mood, the pressures that are placed upon you to conform mean very little. You always were an individual and won't allow your unique qualities to be watered down simply to feed the envious gaze of less imaginative types. You may be more sensitive to criticism than you are willing to show however.

7 SATURDAY
Moon Phase Day 19 • Moon Sign Aries

am ....

pm ....

There are some eye openers about as far as friendship issues are concerned, and not everyone is turning out to be quite as reliable as you might have thought. In love affairs it is likely that you will have to put up with a lull, though there are revealing tendencies about if you are willing to take note of them.

8 SUNDAY
Moon Phase Day 20 • Moon Sign Aries

am ....

pm ....

Back in the social limelight, the place that you most love to be, it may be hard to be as patient as circumstances indicate that you ought to be. In a conversational sense, all you have to do is open your mouth in order to get the accolades that you seek, though some of the compliments that you receive are a little hollow.

← *NEGATIVE TREND*　　　　　*POSITIVE TREND* →

-5	-4	-3	-2	-1		+1	+2	+3	+4	+5
					LOVE					
					MONEY					
					LUCK					
					VITALITY					

9 MONDAY
Moon Phase Day 21 • Moon Sign Aries

am ....

pm ....

It might not be a fortunate aspect to your present nature, especially at the beginning of the week, but you are likely to be feeling in a very quiet mood and only too anxious to retreat from the boring routines that might attend your working life. Even if a physical relocation is not possible you will be travelling in your mind.

10 TUESDAY
Moon Phase Day 22 • Moon Sign Taurus

am ....

pm ....

With Mercury, your ruling planet, now making a triumphant entry into your solar third house, you are about to embark on a very intuitive interlude in your life. This is not a good time for pretensions of any sort and you would be far better viewing both yourself and the world at large, 'Warts and all'.

11 WEDNESDAY
Moon Phase Day 23 • Moon Sign Taurus

am ....

pm ....

There are a couple of planetary aspects that indicate an evasive quality beginning to develop in your nature. Although this might appear to carry some advantages at first, it has to be said that you will not gain in the long-run by evading the truth now and in any case, it isn't possible to fool yourself at all.

12 THURSDAY
Moon Phase Day 24 • Moon Sign Gemini

am ....

pm ....

Along comes the lunar high and suddenly you find that you are galvanised into action. In both personal and practical matters you are now more likely than ever to get your own way and to be able to look fairly at the other person's point of view. Great demands are made of your willpower, and you don't let yourself down.

13 FRIDAY
Moon Phase Day 25 • Moon Sign Gemini

am ....

pm ....

The best area of interaction at the present time is likely to be your love life, and this would be especially true in the case of younger or single Gemini subjects. In a more practical sense you may be doing all you can to finish the week on a positive note, though trying to be a human dynamo won't help.

14 SATURDAY
Moon Phase Day 26 • Moon Sign Cancer

am ....

pm ....

Restless, probably from the very first moment that you get out of bed, how you long to be far away and able to think about things other than the practical necessities of life. Freedom isn't so far away, if you are willing to look at matters objectively. So get your thinking cap on and invent some excitement.

15 SUNDAY
Moon Phase Day 27 • Moon Sign Cancer

am ....

pm ....

High drama in the family really should be avoided if at all possible. Once again you feel the pull of a different destiny and won't want to be held back simply to sort out everyone's inability to see eye to eye. There is enough time in the week ahead to play the diplomat, for now please yourself.

← NEGATIVE TREND							POSITIVE TREND →			
-5	-4	-3	-2	-1		+1	+2	+3	+4	+5
					LOVE					
					MONEY					
					LUCK					
					VITALITY					

16 MONDAY   *Moon Phase Day 28 • Moon Sign Cancer*

am ....

pm ....

A good meeting of minds, perhaps with people that you haven't always managed to understand in the past, can set today apart as
being more interesting than you expected, and more rewarding too.
Whatever you are undertaking, look for pleasure in the way that you
do it, and not merely in how quickly you can get it done.

17 TUESDAY   *Moon Phase Day 0 • Moon Sign Leo*

am ....

pm ....

All powerful Mars takes a trip into your solar fifth house, which
means that for a while you will be calling many of the shots in your
personal life, and especially so where a deeply romantic relationship
is concerned. All the same, you could be making too many demands
on people who are doing their best to please you in any case.

18 WEDNESDAY   *Moon Phase Day 1 • Moon Sign Leo*

am ....

pm ....

There is no doubt that for most Gemini subjects at the present time,
home is the best place to be, even if younger or older people take
some very careful handling. Confidence is on the decrease slightly,
though only enough to make you certain of your actions before you
embark upon them.

19 THURSDAY   *Moon Phase Day 2 • Moon Sign Virgo*

am ....

pm ....

As you look around at all that needs to be done, it could seem that
there is a definite lack of time to fit everything in. You are probably
better at establishing a sensible balance right now than you think,
so that with a little ingenuity it is amazing what becomes possible.

20 FRIDAY
Moon Phase Day 3 • Moon Sign Virgo

am ....

pm ....

Other people are the ones that insist you are in the public eye at the present time, despite the fact that you don't feel especially comfortable to be there. Much of your energy can be put into simply having a good time and that means that something might have to give regarding the practical considerations of life.

21 SATURDAY
Moon Phase Day 4 • Moon Sign Libra

am ....

pm ....

The weekend could easily find you becoming more committed where affairs of the heart are concerned, and even if romance doesn't figure prominently in your life just at the moment, it shouldn't be long before Cupid's darts make a beeline for you. Full co-operation in all practical ventures is vital if you are to make the most of them.

22 SUNDAY
Moon Phase Day 5 • Moon Sign Libra

am ....

pm ....

A diplomatic and softly softly approach is definitely the best way to be dealing with awkward family members today, not that you are likely to have all that much time to think about such things during a period when everyone wants your attention and enlists your support for their own particular cause.

← *NEGATIVE TREND*   *POSITIVE TREND* →

-5	-4	-3	-2	-1		+1	+2	+3	+4	+5
					LOVE					
					MONEY					
					LUCK					
					VITALITY					

142

23 MONDAY

Moon Phase Day 6 • Moon Sign Scorpio

am ....

pm ....

With the Sun now firmly in your solar fourth house of domestic considerations, look for a greater degree of fulfilment becoming possible, thanks to the intervention of the people that you live with and love the most. Close friends are in need of the reassurance that only your quick tongue can provide.

24 TUESDAY

Moon Phase Day 7 • Moon Sign Scorpio

am ....

pm ....

A fairly quiet day, at least when judged by the intensity of recent times. You won't want to be pushed to the forefront of anything unless you can help the situation, all the more reason for keeping a fairly low profile. Meetings and appointments that are planned should not be rushed in any way.

25 WEDNESDAY

Moon Phase Day 8 • Moon Sign Sagittarius

am ....

pm ....

The lunar low brings inevitable small setbacks, though none that are likely to be of any major consequence unless you allow yourself to become depressed by details that are not important and over which you have no control. What cannot be changed at the moment must be endured.

26 THURSDAY

Moon Phase Day 9 • Moon Sign Sagittarius

am ....

pm ....

Bearing in mind the position of the Moon, it would still be wise to be careful how much you are taking on in a practical sense. The problem is that you are liable to run out of emotional and physical steam much more quickly than would usually be the case. Under such circumstances it is all too easy to make mistakes.

27 FRIDAY
Moon Phase Day 10 • Moon Sign Capricorn

am ....

pm ....

Too much anxiety regarding financial matters can be put down partly to the fact that you still haven't managed to respond to the
planetary power surge that follows the lunar low. If you really feel
perturbed, it might be a good idea to seek out some professional advice, if only to put your mind at rest.

28 SATURDAY
Moon Phase Day 11 • Moon Sign Capricorn

am ....

pm ....

Venus in your third house of communication brings favourable news,
relating to someone that you care about a great deal. At home you
are asking for maximum compromise where other people's lives affect your own but maybe you should ask yourself if you are willing to
offer as much in return.

29 SUNDAY
Moon Phase Day 12 • Moon Sign Aquarius

am ....

pm ....

In-depth concentration makes it possible for you to see through to
the heart of any domestic issue that is causing you a degree of
anxiety, though it has to be stressed that you waste the benefits inherent in this most useful Sunday if you squander it in worry. Opt
for a detached concern if you must!

← NEGATIVE TREND						POSITIVE TREND →				
-5	-4	-3	-2	-1		+1	+2	+3	+4	+5
					LOVE					
					MONEY					
					LUCK					
					VITALITY					

30 MONDAY
Moon Phase Day 13 • Moon Sign Aquarius

am ....

pm ....

Do whatever is possible to change routines away from the expected, the very best way to jog your life back into a more positive and less hurried phase. There really is some boredom in store now for those of you who are not willing to take advantage of the opportunities that appear as if by magic.

31 TUESDAY
Moon Phase Day 14 • Moon Sign Aquarius

am ....

pm ....

You may be placed in a taxing role professionally and it will take all the resources that you have at your disposal to get out of it. Putting the finishing touches to situations that you may have considered to be beyond your own control is made easy now and there is every possibility that you will find success handed to you on a plate.

1 WEDNESDAY
Moon Phase Day 15 • Moon Sign Pisces

am ....

pm ....

Personal relationships can be a little irksome, even irritating, though the fact may have more to do with your state of mind than the attitudes of other people. Don't forget that 'live end let live' is your usual attitude to life, and this might be the best adage to bear in mind while you are out of sorts with yourself.

2 THURSDAY
Moon Phase Day 16 • Moon Sign Pisces

am ....

pm ....

Your colleagues appear to be in an uncompromising mood, so it is just as well that your usual tact and diplomacy have returned. This wouldn't be a good time to try and impress people too much and you could gain the most by allowing yourself to listen instead of contributing as much as you generally do.

145

3 FRIDAY
Moon Phase Day 17 • Moon Sign Aries

am ....

pm ....

Social matters are both satisfying and pleasurable. Disagreements that would have caused you more than a little anxiety and worry yesterday don't appear to move you at all now. You still have a need for support, but now it's of an emotional kind, which is why you turn to your loved ones.

4 SATURDAY
Moon Phase Day 18 • Moon Sign Aries

am ....

pm ....

Mars now associated with Jupiter in your solar fifth house is bound to bring a high point in romantic and leisure interests. Some new involvements cannot be ruled out and there is a breath of fresh air coming into your life, at a time when you feel that you need it the most. Encouragement isn't difficult to find.

5 SUNDAY
Moon Phase Day 19 • Moon Sign Aries

am ....

pm ....

Taking the time to look forward, you begin to discover aspects of your own nature that you never really suspected in the recent past. Requests for favours are beginning to come in, and as usual you will be taking the time out to do what you can to help them out. The only situation you ought to think twice about is a request for money.

← NEGATIVE TREND							POSITIVE TREND →			
-5	-4	-3	-2	-1		+1	+2	+3	+4	+5
					LOVE					
					MONEY					
					LUCK					
					VITALITY					

146

SEPTEMBER
1993

YOUR MONTH AT A GLANCE

The twelve numbered boxes represent the important areas in your life.
The key to the numbers you will find beneath the panel. A Sun above
the number indicates that opportunities are around. A Cloud below
the number, that you should be a bit defensive. Nothing above or
below and life will be pretty ordinary.

1	2	3	4	5	6	7	8	9	10	11	12

KEY

1 Strength of Personality
2 Personal Finance
3 Useful Information Gathering
4 Domestic Affairs
5 Pleasure & Romance
6 Effective Work & Health

7 One to One Relationships
8 Questioning, Thinking & Deciding
9 External Influences / Education
10 Career Aspirations
11 Teamwork Activities
12 Unconscious Impulses

SEPTEMBER HIGHS AND LOWS

Here, I show how the rhythm of the Moon will affect you this month.
Like the tide, your energies and abilities will rise and fall with its pattern. When it is above the date line, go-for-it. When it is below the
line you should be resting.

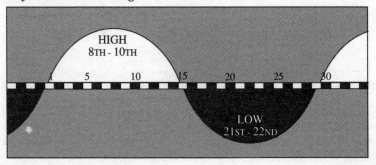

HIGH
8TH - 10TH

5   10   15   20   25   30

LOW
21ST - 22ND

6 MONDAY
Moon Phase Day 20 • Moon Sign Taurus

am ....

pm ....

At the start of a working week that you haven't really prepared
yourself for, you probably won't want to get yourself motivated. As a
result, it is almost certain that you will want to withdraw into yourself. As this wouldn't be a particularly good thing, stay in the main-
stream of events if you can.

7 TUESDAY
Moon Phase Day 21 • Moon Sign Taurus

am ....

pm ....

Feeling pressured from all angles, you presently feel that you are
going nowhere in particular. One benefit of being a Gemini is that
no state of mind lasts nad you never feel the same way for more than
a day or two at a time. If you can't cheer yourself up, you can at
least take heart in what is only a passing phase.

8 WEDNESDAY
Moon Phase Day 22 • Moon Sign Gemini

am ....

pm ....

As the Moon reaches your birth-sign again, life has all the impetus
that it has lacked. At work you are able to find new contacts, and
can make significant gains as a result; though not half as important
as the gains that you can make once your working life is over and
friendship becomes the most important factor.

9 THURSDAY
Moon Phase Day 23 • Moon Sign Gemini

am ....

pm ....

You can afford to take a few risks at present, even if, with your
present shrewd attitude, they tend to be fairly calculated ones. At
your open-hearted and generous best, stay out and about, amidst the
busy routines that so much take your fancy while planetary aspects
are so favourable.

10 FRIDAY
Moon Phase Day 24 • Moon Sign Gemini

am ....

pm ....

There is no point in hanging back once you have made your mind up about anything. The only problem at present is that you don't have the resolve to take your own life in your hands and do whatever comes naturally. There are occasions when life itself knows best and you will find that this is one of them.

11 SATURDAY
Moon Phase Day 25 • Moon Sign Cancer

am ....

pm ....

All leisure and recreational pursuits not only become a possibility in your life now that the weekend has arrived, but an absolute necessity. Mercury is now entering your fifth house and this ensures that your popularity is more than high enough to allow you the greatest degree of influence over other people.

12 SUNDAY
Moon Phase Day 26 • Moon Sign Cancer

am ....

pm ....

Avoid the stifling possibility of boredom by keeping yourself as active as you can. Those Geminis who have chosen this time to take a break or a holiday will already be realising what a good choice you have made. Although you tend to be restless yourself, it is very unlikely that you will be alone in feeling this way.

← NEGATIVE TREND							POSITIVE TREND →				
-5	-4	-3	-2	-1			+1	+2	+3	+4	+5
					LOVE						
					MONEY						
					LUCK						
					VITALITY						

13 MONDAY
Moon Phase Day 27 • Moon Sign Leo

am ....

pm ....

A mental high sends you off, seeking your own roots or looking for other interesting and stimulating interests in or around the vicinity of your home. No matter how dedicated you are in your work, it is the area of your existence that is most likely to take a back seat now that leisure interests are so important.

14 TUESDAY
Moon Phase Day 28 • Moon Sign Leo

am ....

pm ....

People are only too willing to acknowledge not only your achievements but also the brightness of your personality. Tedious jobs really don't take your fancy at the present time and where you cannot avoid them, you can at least approach them with a revolutionary freshness and change their emphasis no end.

15 WEDNESDAY
Moon Phase Day 29 • Moon Sign Virgo

am ....

pm ....

Domestic issues are ever more important as the week goes on. You might want to walk out on certain responsibilities and could be even more restless if it proves impossible for you to delay or cancel them. Emotionally you are up and down and will occasionally find if difficult to see your nearest and dearest's point of view.

16 THURSDAY
Moon Phase Day 0 • Moon Sign Virgo

am ....

pm ....

Present aspects indicate that in a professional sense at least you will find it is much easier to hit upon a 'winning formula' now and having discovered what it is, the best bet is to stick to it. Spirits are generally high, not only for yourself but also in the case of the people that you are mixing with.

17 FRIDAY

Moon Phase Day 1 • Moon Sign Libra

am ....

pm ....

As the working week ends there is little doubt that the Gemini mind is turning towards pleasurable pursuits and the chance to establish a pattern that means having more choice over your own domestic circumstances at least. The behaviour of your closest relatives is difficult to predict, but that only adds to the fun.

18 SATURDAY

Moon Phase Day 2 • Moon Sign Libra

am ....

pm ....

Entering a very instinctive phase, especially when it comes to new acquisitions of any sort, you are unlikely to go wrong if you listen to what your inner mind is telling you. There are things that need doing around the house and, if you are lucky, some willing hands to make the chores less tedious and more fun.

19 SUNDAY

Moon Phase Day 3 • Moon Sign Scorpio

am ....

pm ....

What you seek for now is not a total understanding of every aspect of your life but a more sensible overview. Changes and improvements do have to be considered, though there is nothing to suggest that such considerations should take up every waking hour, or that you have to consider them all at once.

← NEGATIVE TREND   POSITIVE TREND →

-5	-4	-3	-2	-1		+1	+2	+3	+4	+5
					LOVE					
					MONEY					
					LUCK					
					VITALITY					

20 MONDAY   *Moon Phase Day 4 • Moon Sign Scorpio*

am ....

pm ....

Be prepared to slow things down a little because your life can seem
to be like an avalanche, with situations that begin in a relatively in-
significant way and then eventually take on an impetus of their own,
and one that is beyond your control. New skills take some time to
master but are worth the effort.

21 TUESDAY   *Moon Phase Day 5 • Moon Sign Sagittarius*

am ....

pm ....

Some dissatisfaction, with yourself, if not the world at large, is more
or less inevitable as the lunar low begins to manifest itself once
again. However, if you have taken care and know that you are in
the driving seat as far as most situations are concerned, all that you
may notice this time around is a slightly quieter spell.

22 WEDNESDAY   *Moon Phase Day 6 • Moon Sign Sagittarius*

am ....

pm ....

You will be seeking to do all you can to spend time close to home and
to the people that figure the most in your life at the present time. In
a social sense you may have to curtail your activities a little because
there is only so much energy at your disposal and every situation
claims your attention at once.

23 THURSDAY   *Moon Phase Day 7 • Moon Sign Capricorn*

am ....

pm ....

Now that the Sun has changed its position, there is a thirty day
period before you that responds more positively to a consideration of
your domestic circumstances, perhaps made stronger by the fact
that the nights are beginning to draw in somewhat and the fireside
seems to be a much more inviting prospect.

24 FRIDAY
Moon Phase Day 8 • Moon Sign Capricorn

am ....

pm ....

Things are on the move in your solar chart, so that, in addition to the new position of the Sun, Venus is also changing tack and coming to rest in your solar fourth house. The two influences together do make it easier for you to feel fulfilled in a personal achievement sense.

25 SATURDAY
Moon Phase Day 9 • Moon Sign Capricorn

am ....

pm ....

Now it is time to be holding some sensible and, if necessary, protracted discussions about practical and financial matters that have a bearing not only on yourself but also on the people that you live with. The answers that you receive could lead to some head scratching in your desire to reconcile opposing views.

26 SUNDAY
Moon Phase Day 10 • Moon Sign Capricorn

am ....

pm ....

Somehow it is difficult for you to take quite the firm stand that you know to be sensible at the present time, which is why further discussions of a domestic nature could well be best left for a future time and date. Practically everyone that you come across will be impressed by your common sense; everyone that is, except you.

← NEGATIVE TREND								POSITIVE TREND →			
-5	-4	-3	-2	-1			+1	+2	+3	+4	+5
					LOVE						
					MONEY						
					LUCK						
					VITALITY						

27 MONDAY

Moon Phase Day 11• Moon Sign Aquarius

am ....

pm ....

With Mars now entering your solar sixth house and a good deal of
enthusiasm being brought to bear once again on all practical tasks,
you can take a leaf out of the book of the people that you mix with in
a business capacity. You are becoming very co-operative in your behaviour and, together with like minded types, can move mountains.

28 TUESDAY

Moon Phase Day 12 • Moon Sign Pisces

am ....

pm ....

Developments on the career front should do much to raise your
spirits and to make you feel generally more contented with your lot
in life. The attitudes of relatives can be something of a puzzle,
though not for long once you are certain that you have your sensible
head on and are looking at things in a detached way.

29 WEDNESDAY

Moon Phase Day 13 • Moon Sign Pisces

am ....

pm ....

Although you could still sense that there is a gulf between yourself
and your partner, or perhaps a close friend, this is not an insur-
mountable problem and should not be allowed to interfere with the
general progress that is possible on this most positive of days.
Financial news that you receive is likely to be very pleasing.

30 THURSDAY

Moon Phase Day 14 • Moon Sign Pisces

am ....

pm ....

Socially restless, though quite contented in other ways, what you
need at the moment is to be looking towards the possibility of new
out of work activities to really stretch you in ways that have not
been possible or advisable in the recent past. Where others are concerned, your convictions are especially strong at the moment.

1 FRIDAY
Moon Phase Day 15 • Moon Sign Aries

am ....

pm ....

News comes in regarding your work and circumstances related to it that are likely to make life just a little more comfortable as far as your own circumstances are affected by it. In many ways you are preoccupied with projects that are close to your own heart at the present time and won't have much time for social chit-chat.

2 SATURDAY
Moon Phase Day 16 • Moon Sign Aries

am ....

pm ....

The bright lights of a much improved social world now begin to beckon and make you realise that, despite your earlier considerations to the contrary, you are not going to be a doremouse this winter. Already you are lining up a number of new possibilities, some of which will be associated with your personal life.

3 SUNDAY
Moon Phase Day 17 • Moon Sign Taurus

am ....

pm ....

Meetings and encounters of a typically Geminian type can predominate on a Sunday that appears to be based exclusively on your need to mix and mingle. Just about anyone that comes along is grist to the mill of your quick and keen intellect. Other people appear only too willing to let you into their secrets.

← NEGATIVE TREND						POSITIVE TREND →				
-5	-4	-3	-2	-1		+1	+2	+3	+4	+5
					LOVE					
					MONEY					
					LUCK					
					VITALITY					

OCTOBER
1993

YOUR MONTH AT A GLANCE

The twelve numbered boxes represent the important areas in your life.
The key to the numbers you will find beneath the panel. A Sun above
the number indicates that opportunities are around. A Cloud below
the number, that you should be a bit defensive. Nothing above or
below and life will be pretty ordinary.

1	2	3	4	5	6 ☀	7	8	9 ☁	10	11 ☀	12 ☁

KEY

1 Strength of Personality	7 One to One Relationships
2 Personal Finance	8 Questioning, Thinking & Deciding
3 Useful Information Gathering	9 External Influences / Education
4 Domestic Affairs	10 Career Aspirations
5 Pleasure & Romance	11 Teamwork Activities
6 Effective Work & Health	12 Unconscious Impulses

OCTOBER HIGHS AND LOWS

Here, I show how the rhythm of the Moon will affect you this month.
Like the tide, your energies and abilities will rise and fall with its pattern. When it is above the date line, go-for-it. When it is below the
line you should be resting.

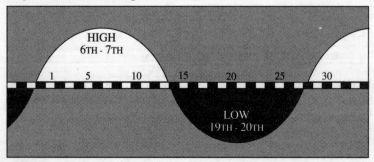

HIGH
6TH - 7TH

LOW
19TH - 20TH

4 MONDAY   *Moon Phase Day 18 • Moon Sign Taurus*

am ....

pm ....

Comfort and a sense of security are no doubt on your mind at the start of this new week, which is why you might be thinking in terms of feathering your own nest in a practical sense and in the eyes of the people that are so important to you. Don't try too hard to make an impression though; you already have.

5 TUESDAY   *Moon Phase Day 19 • Moon Sign Taurus*

am ....

pm ....

With the lunar high now only hours away, you have an unbroken period between now and the weekend that makes for some very positive moves on your behalf. Because you appear to be so shrewd, there is little chance that anyone would be trying to pull the wool over your eyes or to confuse you with details.

6 WEDNESDAY   *Moon Phase Day 20 • Moon Sign Gemini*

am ....

pm ....

It is likely to be the practical considerations of your life that are so much assisted by the lunar high this month, probably because you have already set out on a campaign to make things run more smoothly in this department of your life in any case. Confront people about important issues if you feel really strongly.

7 THURSDAY   *Moon Phase Day 21 • Moon Sign Gemini*

am ....

pm ....

You would do well to avoid rivalry becoming an issue today, not that it is likely to be you that is making an issue out of situations that you would consider to be relatively unimportant. All the same, you may have to defend yourself, an inevitable part of being a gregarious and go-getting Gemini on occasions.

8 FRIDAY
Moon Phase Day 22 • Moon Sign Cancer

am ....

pm ....

Things should be turning out well concerning financial transactions and general wealth in the longer-term sense. Investments of one sort or another could require careful handling at first, and the advice of an expert should not be ruled out as a possibility. Stay open-minded when considering the behaviour of friends.

9 SATURDAY
Moon Phase Day 23 • Moon Sign Cancer

am ....

pm ....

Don't forget at this time that you do need interests outside of your work, a fact that may be brought home to you by the social quality of the weekend that you are now embarking upon. Your ability to change direction at a moment's notice is a source of some wonder to the people that you are dealing with, though not to you.

10 SUNDAY
Moon Phase Day 24 • Moon Sign Leo

am ....

pm ....

Situations of confrontation really should be avoided at all cost today. What you need is a mixture of something interesting to do and an equal measure of peace and quiet. What you don't need are other people telling you how you ought to behave or gathering round to enlist your support for a pointless family squabble.

← NEGATIVE TREND　　　　　　　*POSITIVE TREND →*

-5	-4	-3	-2	-1			+1	+2	+3	+4	+5
				▓	LOVE						
				▓	MONEY						
					LUCK		▓				
					VITALITY		▓	▓			

158

11 MONDAY
Moon Phase Day 25 • Moon Sign Leo

am ....

pm ....

Long-standing relationships of one sort or another may well be something that you are giving a measure of consideration to at the present time. Not everyone behaves in quite the way that you expect, a fact that can cause some annoyance and frustration. It might be best to put such thoughts on one side for now.

12 TUESDAY
Moon Phase Day 26 • Moon Sign Leo

am ....

pm ....

You won't get anywhere at all if you allow important matters to be left to chance because if ever there was a time to take your destiny in your own hands, this is it. Be prepared to have a good time socially as the bright lights beckon and you find yourself in exactly the right frame of mind to make the most out of encounters.

13 WEDNESDAY
Moon Phase Day 27 • Moon Sign Virgo

am ....

pm ....

Secrets and security are two possibilities that could be taking up far more of your hours than is really healthy for a forward looking, fast thinking Gemini subject such as yourself. There is a darker and more secretive side to your nature, though this is not the time for allowing it to rule you.

14 THURSDAY
Moon Phase Day 28 • Moon Sign Virgo

am ....

pm ....

All situations of love and romance have the chance to flourish at the present time as you get yourself in the mood for wine and roses. This could be an ideal period to be thinking up some special treat for the person who figures the most in your life, or for looking for new romance if you are a single Gemini.

15 FRIDAY
Moon Phase Day 0 • Moon Sign Libra

am ....

pm ....

Finding yourself to be the centre of attraction in the eyes of just about everyone, you have the ability to make people sit up and take notice of you to a greater extent than at almost any other time this month. People from the past come into your life again and make you want to turn the clock back somehow.

16 SATURDAY
Moon Phase Day 1 • Moon Sign Libra

am ....

pm ....

It occurs to you now to spend a little time looking at the way that you relate to other people, though it is uncertain how necessary this type of thinking is to a person who instinctively knows how to adapt to others. You should be in for a very sociable weekend, even if there are some miserable types about.

17 SUNDAY
Moon Phase Day 2 • Moon Sign Scorpio

am ....

pm ....

For those amongst you who are not settled in a personal sense, and especially Gemini people to whom personal difficulties have been a fact of life, there are now possibilities about quite soon, perhaps even right now if you keep your eyes open and can manage to push your credibility through the roof.

← *NEGATIVE TREND*   *POSITIVE TREND* →

-5	-4	-3	-2	-1		+1	+2	+3	+4	+5
					LOVE					
					MONEY					
					LUCK					
					VITALITY					

18 MONDAY   *Moon Phase Day 3 • Moon Sign Scorpio*

am ....

pm ....

This may not turn out to be the most positive start to a week that
you have had. The lunar low is not very far away and so it isn't likely that you would be feeling that you could push any buses over.
Not that you have to be working flat out all the time; sometimes sit-
ting and thinking can be just as important.

19 TUESDAY   *Moon Phase Day 4 • Moon Sign Sagittarius*

am ....

pm ....

Stay open to the subterranean influences that you, probably more
than anyone, can tune into if you set your mind to the task. In
every way at present, it isn't what people are telling you that is particularly important now but the way that you respond to words that
are not being said. Intuition has rarely been stronger.

20 WEDNESDAY   *Moon Phase Day 5 • Moon Sign Sagittarius*

am ....

pm ....

Think through all personal searches for greater development
carefully before you decide that the time is right to put plans into action. There is little point in causing confrontations with others
today, no matter how much their attitudes annoy you. You just
aren't in the mood to be arguing.

21 THURSDAY   *Moon Phase Day 6 • Moon Sign Capricorn*

am ....

pm ....

You could find it necessary to spell out your intentions more than
once today, especially if you are dealing with people who do not have
your ability to see the heart of matters. In a professional sense you
will be expected to make the first move and to be sure that obstacles
are cleared away first.

22 FRIDAY
Moon Phase Day 7 • Moon Sign Capricorn

am ....

pm ....

The wind of change is blowing, mainly because your level of energy in on the up again and you just can't stand the thought of your life standing as still as it seems to have done for the last few days. There are some unique individuals about now and since you are quite unusual yourself, you will be seeking them out.

23 SATURDAY
Moon Phase Day 8 • Moon Sign Aquarius

am ....

pm ....

'Forcing issues' is something that you won't be able to prevent yourself from doing during the month that lies ahead, for now you have the Sun in your solar sixth house. You become a frontier person to a much greater extent and gain more from the ability and desire to break new ground.

24 SUNDAY
Moon Phase Day 9 • Moon Sign Aquarius

am ....

pm ....

Doing all that you can to make other people feel comfortable, it would be just as well to realise that you are not responsible for their plight in the first place. Nevertheless, it is your desire at the present time to do what you can for a number of individuals who you consider to be in genuine need.

← *NEGATIVE TREND*							*POSITIVE TREND* →			
-5	-4	-3	-2	-1			+1	+2	+3	+4	+5
					LOVE						
					MONEY						
					LUCK						
					VITALITY						

25 MONDAY   *Moon Phase Day 10 • Moon Sign Pisces*

am ....

pm ....

There are delays to be considered, particularly in a workaday sense, though nothing that should prove to be any more than a temporary setback, now that you are in such a positive and assertive mood. Colleagues can be very irritating and might even appear to be behaving in a deliberately awkward way.

26 TUESDAY   *Moon Phase Day 11 • Moon Sign Pisces*

am ....

pm ....

With apparently dramatic events unfolding on all sides, you steer your way through potentially troubled waters like the time served pilot that you are. The period is an exciting one, and there are no lack of people around to take you out of yourself. A word of caution though: don't push yourself too hard in a physical sense.

27 WEDNESDAY   *Moon Phase Day 12 • Moon Sign Pisces*

am ....

pm ....

Some of your best laid plans will be subject to a degree of in-depth thought now and could need some degree of manipulation if they are to become the sort of realities that you had hoped. On a more positive note, your love life is offered a boost and personal relationships at home will also be showing some amusing diversions.

28 THURSDAY   *Moon Phase Day 13 • Moon Sign Aries*

am ....

pm ....

Back on 'terms' with people that haven't been easy to deal with for quite a while, you are in a rather pensive mood and anxious to look and see what makes other people behave in the way that they do. It isn't certain that you will find the answers that you are looking for, though simply having searched is what makes you tick.

163

29 FRIDAY

Moon Phase Day 14 • Moon Sign Aries

am ....

pm ....

Because you are generally wrapped up in the practical matters that life throws into your path today, there is a chance that you will fail to notice the very favourable attention that is being paid to you by someone that may well hold you in especially high esteem. How you choose to react is really dependant on how free you consider youself.

30 SATURDAY

Moon Phase Day 15 • Moon Sign Taurus

am ....

pm ....

After a busy and sometimes over complicated week, there is a chance that you will not opt for every diversion that is on offer in a social sense. In the case of family feuds, you would not find a better time to be burying the hatchet once and for all, though you may find it hard to make a friend of the person concerned.

31 SUNDAY

Moon Phase Day 16 • Moon Sign Taurus

am ....

pm ....

It is far too easy to scatter your energies and dissipate your natural talents today, during what should be a quiet and contemplative sort of Sunday. If you are getting out and about, your preference is likely to be for the top of a low hill or somewhere within the sight of a rolling sea.

NOVEMBER
1993

YOUR MONTH AT A GLANCE

The twelve numbered boxes represent the important areas in your life. The key to the numbers you will find beneath the panel. A Sun above the number indicates that opportunities are around. A Cloud below the number, that you should be a bit defensive. Nothing above or below and life will be pretty ordinary.

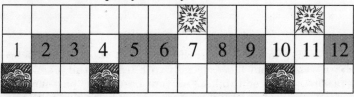

KEY

1 Strength of Personality
2 Personal Finance
3 Useful Information Gathering
4 Domestic Affairs
5 Pleasure & Romance
6 Effective Work & Health

7 One to One Relationships
8 Questioning, Thinking & Deciding
9 External Influences / Education
10 Career Aspirations
11 Teamwork Activities
12 Unconscious Impulses

NOVEMBER HIGHS AND LOWS

Here, I show how the rhythm of the Moon will affect you this month. Like the tide, your energies and abilities will rise and fall with its pattern. When it is above the date line, go-for-it. When it is below the line you should be resting.

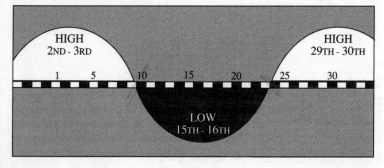

1 MONDAY
Moon Phase Day 17 • Moon Sign Taurus

am ....

pm ....

This is an excellent start to the month, with good fortune more than likely to shine on you, and in a number of different ways. Relationships are working out especially well and you can follow on from chance encounters or a re-kindling of past meetings. All the same you will not be looking back at all.

2 TUESDAY
Moon Phase Day 18 • Moon Sign Gemini

am ....

pm ....

The lunar high comes along at the very start of the month to bring an extra boost to your life, especially with regard to all practical considerations. Inspired thinking on your part in the past now turns out to have been more useful than you probably thought at the time. Don't be melodramatic in your personal attachments.

3 WEDNESDAY
Moon Phase Day 19 • Moon Sign Gemini

am ....

pm ....

Time is still right to put all your plans into action, and this is especially true in the case of all workaday considerations which are likely to be flexible enough to allow your input. Little problems that may have beset your most important relationships respond well to some careful thinking now.

4 THURSDAY
Moon Phase Day 20 • Moon Sign Cancer

am ....

pm ....

Financial rewards are likely, once again, not because of what you are doing now, but on account of the effort that you have been putting into life over the last few weeks. Words of encouragement are especially important to you at the moment, mainly because of where they are coming from.

5 FRIDAY
Moon Phase Day 21 • Moon Sign Cancer

am ....

pm ....

The softer the approach that you adopt tomorrow, the better the result. Before you can really get things moving in the direction that you want them to go in from a practical point of view, you will have to shake people into action. This is best achieved by using a psychological approach to your encounters.

6 SATURDAY
Moon Phase Day 22 • Moon Sign Cancer

am ....

pm ....

It seems that you feel a lot more like yourself than you have done for a day or two, though in order to be certain, it would first be necessary to know what you usually are. General changes to your nature are an inevitable consequence of the next couple of months and they take a while to finally settle down.

7 SUNDAY
Moon Phase Day 23 • Moon Sign Leo

am ....

pm ....

Relations and friends try to pull you in two different directions right now, and having decided what you want to do with your Sunday, it is important that you leave others in no doubt as to your preferences. If people still insist on being awkward, it might be a good idea to spend some time on your own.

← *NEGATIVE TREND*   *POSITIVE TREND* →

-5	-4	-3	-2	-1		+1	+2	+3	+4	+5
					LOVE					
					MONEY					
					LUCK					
					VITALITY					

8 MONDAY

Moon Phase Day 24 • Moon Sign Leo

am ....

pm ....

Good news comes along, related in some way to personal or professional issues. It could be hard to separate the various spheres of your life at present, since all areas are inter-related in some way. The pace of everyday situations can leave you feeling a little dizzy and wanting a rest.

9 TUESDAY

Moon Phase Day 25 • Moon Sign Virgo

am ....

pm ....

Mars now enters your solar seventh house, and it becomes ever more difficult to make the sort of compromise that is necessary. The closer people are to you, the more demanding they seem to be, though your own view of life is somewhat distorted and can be just as difficult for others to deal with.

10 WEDNESDAY

Moon Phase Day 26 • Moon Sign Virgo

am ....EXSAT...

pm ....

The solar picture is now beginning to change quite significantly as Jupiter settles into your sixth house. This ushers in a period of quite extraordinary possibility for many children of Mercury, especially related to work and your constant need for security in a more personal sense. Look for as many fresh starts as you can find.

11 THURSDAY

Moon Phase Day 27 • Moon Sign Libra

am ....

pm ....

The trio of changes in your chart is now completed with Venus entering your solar sixth house. Most career prospects should be going your way and you are probably enjoying the positive cut and thrust of the working scene. There are quite definite connections between apparently unrelated areas of your life.

168

12 FRIDAY
Moon Phase Day 28 • Moon Sign Libra

am ....

pm ....

Now you can really be experiencing the best of both worlds at a time when you are happy in your work and with the general contentment that is obvious in your home life. The only problem could lie in taking the situation for granted and losing touch with matters as a result.

13 SATURDAY
Moon Phase Day 0 • Moon Sign Scorpio

am ....

pm ....

The weekend finds you more than anxious to make the most of any situation that appears to be going your way. There are tests of strength concerning your determination and that of the people that you live with, though these are really no more than a rattling of sabres. In the main, life should be smooth and steady.

14 SUNDAY
Moon Phase Day 1 • Moon Sign Scorpio

am ....

pm ....

Personal developments can take something of a back seat, and friendship is the most important factor of a busy, though not too exciting day. The quietness of life isn't a problem to you however and you might even choose to spend some time on your own, as a counter to the hectic quality of the working week.

← NEGATIVE TREND							POSITIVE TREND →				
-5	-4	-3	-2	-1			+1	+2	+3	+4	+5
					LOVE						
					MONEY						
					LUCK						
					VITALITY						

15 MONDAY

Moon Phase Day 2 • Moon Sign Sagittarius

am ....

pm ....

Starting the week on a lunar low doesn't offer you quite the incentive that you might have desired. As usual at such times, this is an interlude for allowing life to work its quiet miracles within your nature. Not that this means that you are unable to achieve at least some of your most cherished objectives.

16 TUESDAY

Moon Phase Day 3 • Moon Sign Sagittarius

am ....

pm ....

In your daily routines it would be far better now to do a few things completely and efficiently than to try and complete a mountain of tasks and fail to do justice to any of them. There can be one or two disappointments on account of the behaviour of friends, so it would be best not to expect too much.

17 WEDNESDAY

Moon Phase Day 4 • Moon Sign Capricorn

am .... *EXEAT* ....

pm ....

The pendulum swings and you find all the energy that you lacked yesterday is now at your disposal again. In your work there is a certain decisiveness around you that will make others only too willing to fall behind your plans. Criticism is a possibility but it won't bother you at present.

18 THURSDAY

Moon Phase Day 5 • Moon Sign Capricorn

am ....

pm ....

If things have been allowed to slide on the home front, especially with regard to the attitudes of other family members, you had better get your thinking cap on and deal with the situation as soon as you can. You can be certain that you have everyone's best interests at heart, even if they doubt the fact.

19 FRIDAY

Moon Phase Day 6 • Moon Sign Aquarius

am ....

pm ....

In some social sense you get the impression that you have fallen out of favour, though in all probability you are just being too sensitive. It is fair to suggest that you may have inadvertently upset a particularly difficult person with something that you said, though that is a matter that you should easily be able to rectify.

20 SATURDAY

Moon Phase Day 7 • Moon Sign Aquarius

am ....

pm ....

The emphasis now really does have to be on your own life and the things that seem to be most important to you. There are plenty of individuals who are only too willing to tell you how you ought to behave and on occasions you will have to put them straight. In everything stay calm, cool and collected.

21 SUNDAY

Moon Phase Day 8 • Moon Sign Aquarius

am ....

pm ....

It is very important to register the impression that you are making on other people at the moment, even though it may only be in a social and not a business sense. What you require is more confidence and there is nowhere better to find it than in the knowledge that others find you entertaining and amusing.

← *NEGATIVE TREND*   *POSITIVE TREND* →

-5	-4	-3	-2	-1		+1	+2	+3	+4	+5
					LOVE					
					MONEY					
					LUCK					
					VITALITY					

22 MONDAY

Moon Phase Day 9 • Moon Sign Pisces

am ....

pm .... CUP Match. ....

You are inclined to play down your own accomplishments today, in favour of telling those around you how clever they are being. All the same it is very important not to hide your light under a bushel at a time when people of influence are apt to be following your actions very carefully indeed.

23 TUESDAY

Moon Phase Day 10 • Moon Sign Pisces

am ....

pm ....

With the Sun now in your solar seventh house, most of your attention is being expounded on work and associated topics. It is very important to you that you are aware of your successes, whilst your colleagues are willing to indicate how important you are in the general scheme of things.

24 WEDNESDAY

Moon Phase Day 11 • Moon Sign Aries

am ....

pm ....

Not all the ideas that you have at the present time are doomed to end up on the scrap-heap of experience. On the contrary, the unique quality of your mind can create some interesting and quite revolutionary plans and schemes, which may not be half as far fetched as would appear to be the case at first.

25 THURSDAY

Moon Phase Day 12 • Moon Sign Aries

am ....

pm .... CUP Match (RUGBY) ....

In the eyes of the people that you mix with the most, your profile is growing, which makes you the one that is being sought out for advice on just about every topic under the sun. Because you are feeling so generous it would be difficult for you to deny anyone the time that they demand of you.

26 FRIDAY
Moon Phase Day 13 • Moon Sign Aries

am ....

pm ....

There are not many periods when gregarious Gemini chooses to sit in a corner and think, though you find yourself in the right mood to be doing so right now. Not that anything specific is likely to be bothering you; it's simply the case that you are feeling pensive and can gain much by indulging in a little meditation.

27 SATURDAY
Moon Phase Day 14 • Moon Sign Taurus

am ....

pm ....

Having established a better line of communication with your own subconscious, you now decide upon some quite unique methods of expressing the way that you are feeling. The waters of your mind are running deeper than usual, so you shouldn't be surprised that your friends find this interlude difficult to understand.

28 SUNDAY
Moon Phase Day 15 • Moon Sign Taurus

am ....

pm ....

It may not be the time of the year that you enjoy the most, though that shouldn't prevent you from getting out and about today. The last thing that you need after yesterday is to be spending too much time on your own, and be it jobs around the house or a visit to see friends, you have to be amidst the throng.

← NEGATIVE TREND						POSITIVE TREND →				
-5	-4	-3	-2	-1		+1	+2	+3	+4	+5
					LOVE					
					MONEY					
					LUCK					
					VITALITY					

29 MONDAY

Moon Phase Day 16 • Moon Sign Gemini

am ....

pm ....

It has taken some time for your nature to reach its peak again but with the aid of the lunar high, commencing today, you really begin to feel like a true Gemini again. The start of the working week merely means another set of challenges that you will be only too happy to take on board, and the kind of interaction that you love.

30 TUESDAY

Moon Phase Day 17 • Moon Sign Gemini

am ....

pm ....

You will find that it is in matters emotional that the present position of the moon is of most use to you. Chances are that you feel more generally settled than has been possible for a week of two and will be looking for nothing more inside yourself than you are able to offer all the time. A good way to end the calendar month!

1 WEDNESDAY

Moon Phase Day 18 • Moon Sign Gemini

am ....

pm ....

It is a case of 'never a dull moment' in your life as you embark on the last month of 1993. Though you could not class this as a quiet and peaceful sort of day, it has a magic all of its own for those children of Mercury who are looking for action in abundance. Try to get on top of old and outmoded habits.

2 THURSDAY

Moon Phase Day 19 • Moon Sign Cancer

am ....

pm ....

Things take time to get right, though you ought to have discovered by now that time is a commodity that can be stretched and altered to suit your particular needs. In some ways you are quite willing to seek out expert advice, a fact that could be of tremendous importance where a new and important venture is concerned.

3 FRIDAY
Moon Phase Day 20 • Moon Sign Cancer

am ....

pm ....

Establishing a harmonious and long lasting co-operation with the individuals that you work with, it is slightly more difficult to persuade people to fall in line in a domestic sense. It's a time to put your ideas across as calmly and rationally as you can, and to look out for the happiness that romantic prospects can bring.

4 SATURDAY
Moon Phase Day 21 • Moon Sign Leo

am ....

pm ....

Your presence is commanding now, and those of you who work during the weekend can make significant gains as a result. Unfortunately the same cannot be said to be true in a domestic sense, because the people that you live amongst are far less likely to be taking any notice of your dynamism.

5 SUNDAY
Moon Phase Day 22 • Moon Sign Leo

am ....

pm ....

A slow and quite uninspiring start is your lot today, but that doesn't have to be the way that things end up. Partners and loved ones now appear to be much more willing to back you up, whatever it is that you have to say. Social trends are set for some interesting encounters, especially if you are willing to be out and about.

← NEGATIVE TREND								POSITIVE TREND →				
-5	-4	-3	-2	-1				+1	+2	+3	+4	+5
				▓	LOVE							
					MONEY			▓	▓			
					LUCK			▓				
					VITALITY			▓				

DECEMBER
1993

YOUR MONTH AT A GLANCE

The twelve numbered boxes represent the important areas in your life. The key to the numbers you will find beneath the panel. A Sun above the nomber indicates that opportunities are around. A Cloud below the number, that you should be a bit defensive. Nothing above or below and life will be pretty ordinary.

1	2	3	4	5	6	7	8	9	10	11	12

KEY

1 Strength of Personality
2 Personal Finance
3 Useful Information Gathering
4 Domestic Affairs
5 Pleasure & Romance
6 Effective Work & Health

7 One to One Relationships
8 Questioning, Thinking & Deciding
9 External Influences / Education
10 Career Aspirations
11 Teamwork Activities
12 Unconscious Impulses

DECEMBER HIGHS AND LOWS

Here, I show how the rhythm of the Moon will affect you this month. Like the tide, your energies and abilities will rise and fall with its pattern. When it is above the date line, go-for-it. When it is below the line you should be resting.

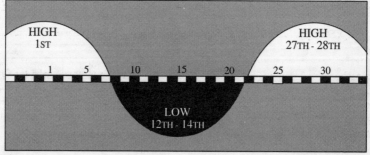

6 MONDAY   *Moon Phase Day 23 • Moon Sign Virgo*

am ....

pm ....

Mixing up professional and domestic matters is one of the worst things that you can allow yourself to do at this point in time, in fact it would be quite sensible to make certain that you only deal with situations one at a time, no matter what they may relate to. The multi-faceted Gemini takes a back seat for the next couple of days.

7 TUESDAY   *Moon Phase Day 24 • Moon Sign Virgo*

am ....

pm ....

It is amazing how reasonable everyone appears to be now, though there is no doubt that your own frame of mind has something to do with the situation. For those of you who have allowed personal upsets to cloud your judgements recently, now is the time to climb out of the ditch and see the amazing landscape that life has created.

8 WEDNESDAY   *Moon Phase Day 25 • Moon Sign Libra*

am ....

pm ....

Encouraged by others, you surge forward in a number of different ways, the only potential problem being that you are bound to do more than is really good for you and can cause yourself some fatigue as a result. Routines are a drag, which is why you will be leaving them to others whenever you can.

9 THURSDAY   *Moon Phase Day 26 • Moon Sign Libra*

am ....

pm ....

Unlike your general self, there is a possibility that you could be far too self-indulgent at the moment. On the other hand this could be a reflection of your present generosity, though on this occasion turned in on yourself. Either way, it is something to guard against and can only cause problems later.

10 FRIDAY
Moon Phase Day 27 • Moon Sign Scorpio

am ....

pm ....

You expect the best from life now and, true to form, you are not likely to be let down. There will be a price to pay if you are less than sensitive in your dealings with other people, particularly your partner or a loved one who needs special consideration. Mercury in your seventh house 'softens' your responses.

11 SATURDAY
Moon Phase Day 28 • Moon Sign Scorpio

am ....

pm ....

Information comes rolling in from a variety of different directions and keeps you at the forefront of events. Socially you look forward to the interaction of an interesting and rewarding period and may be getting to grips with the implications of the impending festive season.

12 SUNDAY
Moon Phase Day 29 • Moon Sign Sagittarius

am ....

pm ....

Things are bound to be quieter as the lunar low pays you the last visit of the year, though you should be pleased to get it out of the way before Christmas arrives and demands so much of your resources. Today is better for social activity and the company of people that you probably don't get to see too often.

← NEGATIVE TREND							POSITIVE TREND →				
-5	-4	-3	-2	-1			+1	+2	+3	+4	+5
					LOVE						
					MONEY						
					LUCK						
					VITALITY						

13 MONDAY   *Moon Phase Day 0 • Moon Sign Sagittarius*

am ....

pm ....

It isn't you that holds the key to your own success at the moment and if you want to know where it really lies, you will have to embark on a journey of discovery within your own mind. It is a shame that you cannot make a real journey of some sort too because it would dissipate some of your present restlessness.

14 TUESDAY   *Moon Phase Day 1 • Moon Sign Sagittarius*

am ....

pm ....

You should have been an actor! Certainly there is nobody to touch you when it comes to playing the right sort of role to meet the drama that life is offering you at any point in time. Today it is comedy, though with just a hint of melodrama thrown in for good luck. Opt for some relaxation in the evening.

15 WEDNESDAY   *Moon Phase Day 2 • Moon Sign Capricorn*

am ....

pm ....

Life is hectic, with barely a moment to think about the chaotic social round that stands before you in only a week or so. Half the problem might be that you are already on the move and will expect to burn the candle at both ends from now until the start of January. Take some advice. Think again!

16 THURSDAY   *Moon Phase Day 3 • Moon Sign Capricorn*

am ....

pm ....

All associations of change and travel once again begin to figure significantly in your patterns of thought. Because you are so tied down by responsibility and circumstance, in your head is the place that such desire for fresh fields and pastures new are likely to stay. There is nothing to prevent you from stretching your imagination.

17 FRIDAY
Moon Phase Day 4 • Moon Sign Aquarius

am ....

pm ....

Get your head together with like-minded people and sort out a series of problems that other people have clearly been avoiding. You have great presence of mind, together with the sort of diplomacy that can achieve the impossible. Most important of all, people want to hear what you have to say.

18 SATURDAY
Moon Phase Day 5 • Moon Sign Aquarius

am ....

pm ....

Any rivalry that stands around you at the present time is likely to be of a very healthy sort and since you show no signs of being anxious regarding your own abilities, you will be quite happy to lock antlers with just about anyone. If you win this little contest, it is by outwitting your rival.

19 SUNDAY
Moon Phase Day 6 • Moon Sign Pisces

am ....

pm ....

Progress begins to be much smoother and less periodical than has been the case recently, always a good thing in the lives of Geminis, who are inclined to live their lives on the swing of a pendulum. Look out for some subtle but very interesting signposts that can lead to a magical romantic interlude if you take note of them.

← NEGATIVE TREND							POSITIVE TREND →			
-5	-4	-3	-2	-1			+1	+2	+3	+4	+5
					LOVE						
					MONEY						
					LUCK						
					VITALITY						

20 MONDAY
Moon Phase Day 7 • Moon Sign Pisces

am ....

pm ....

With Mars now taking a trip into your eighth house, it's off with the old and on with the new, though slightly in advance of the new year as far as you are concerned. Some of the practical changes that you want to make will have to wait until after Christmas, but that is no reason why planning should wait too.

21 TUESDAY
Moon Phase Day 8 • Moon Sign Pisces

am ....

pm ....

Even though you really want to co-operate as much as you can there is still a danger that your mode of thinking will alienate other people and that you may fail to reach the sort of understanding that you know to be so important to you now. Life is full of characters and you come across your fair share.

22 WEDNESDAY
Moon Phase Day 9 • Moon Sign Aries

am ....

pm ....

With the Sun now about to enter your eighth house, you are fortunate in being able to embark upon a number of changes within your own life at just the right time of the year. You feel determined to make things work for you in ways that have proved to be difficult this year, though the future is very much an open book.

23 THURSDAY
Moon Phase Day 10 • Moon Sign Aries

am ....

pm ....

Mercury in your solar seventh house should make this an excellent period in all the ways that really count. Only a couple of days away from Christmas, your sensitivity is especially high and you find it easy to adapt your own plans to include those of your loved ones. A romantic Christmas is likely for Geminis.

24 FRIDAY

Moon Phase Day 11 • Moon Sign Taurus

am ....

pm ....

Busy, busy child of Mercury, trying to fit more into a single Christmas Eve than most people could get out of half a dozen. As long as your energy lasts out you are in for a riotous and very fulfilling time, though chances are that you will soon flop once the evening comes along. Younger people find words to touch you.

25 SATURDAY

Moon Phase Day 12 • Moon Sign Taurus

am ....

pm ....

Strangely enough you are likely to be a little quieter for Christmas itself and could content yourself with a back seat, allowing other people to make some of the running. What you won't want to do is watch 'The Sound Of Music' yet again, so family visiting could be the preferred option.

26 SUNDAY

Moon Phase Day 13 • Moon Sign Taurus

am ....

pm ....

Only a matter of hours away from your lunar high, now you really get down to having a good time, in the way that only a true Gemini subject knows how to do. Being the life and soul of any party, and even arranging some of them, there is little time to draw breath and everything to play for in terms of excitement.

← *NEGATIVE TREND*   *POSITIVE TREND* →

-5	-4	-3	-2	-1		+1	+2	+3	+4	+5
					LOVE					
					MONEY					
					LUCK					
					VITALITY					

27 MONDAY   *Moon Phase Day 14 • Moon Sign Gemini*

am ....

pm ....

People are more than willing to share their confidences with you at the moment, so much so that it could be difficult to get away from them. Comfort and security look inviting if you are at home today, that is until you become restless again and start to wonder where you can go next to break the monotony.

28 TUESDAY   *Moon Phase Day 15 • Moon Sign Gemini*

am ....

pm ....

An intense emotional involvement makes you feel really alive and you tingle all over with the sheer excitement of what life has to offer you. There is little chance of concentrating on practical considerations so you may as well give yourself to the mood the is taking you over and enjoy what life is saying.

29 WEDNESDAY   *Moon Phase Day 16 • Moon Sign Cancer*

am ....

pm ....

Your charisma is turned up to full power and that makes you very attractive in the eyes of others, especially members of the opposite sex. Unfortunately this could lead to one or two complications at the moment and is something that a few of you would want to avoid at all cost. Not a good day for resolutions.

30 THURSDAY   *Moon Phase Day 17 • Moon Sign Cancer*

am ....

pm ....

Don't take offers for granted, especially if they are related to cash in any way. In terms of your relationships with other people you are still in a fairly commanding position, particularly since you can put your message across so well. Opt for quietness later in the day if you have a choice.

31 FRIDAY

Moon Phase Day 18 • Moon Sign Leo

am ....

pm ....

Well, it's been quite a year, and you will be happy now to set your mind on the possibilities that stand before you so tantalisingly. Discussions can mean a great deal today and you won't have to take time out to plan resolutions; you already know where you are going, and how to get there..

← NEGATIVE TREND						POSITIVE TREND →				
-5	-4	-3	-2	-1		+1	+2	+3	+4	+5
					LOVE					
					MONEY					
					LUCK					
					VITALITY					

RISING SIGNS
for GEMINI

Look along the top to find your date of birth, and down the side f
hour (or two) if appropriate for Summer Time.

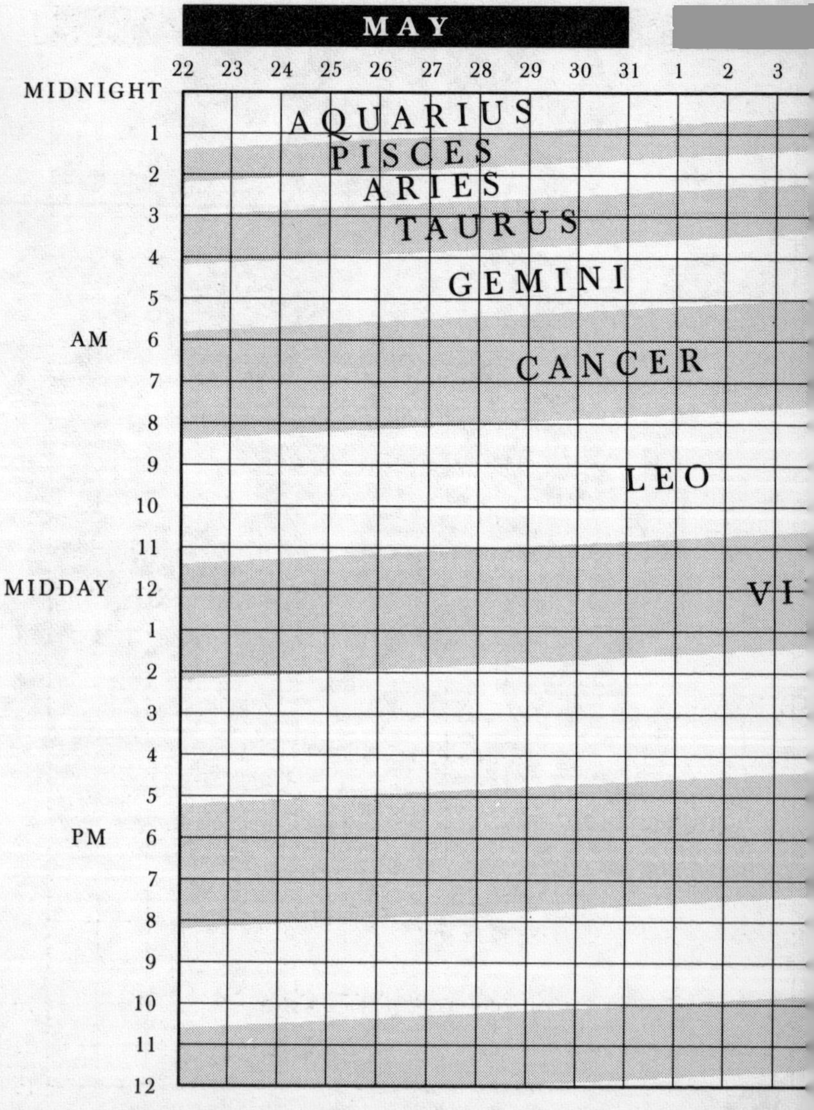

					MAY							
	22	23	24	25	26	27	28	29	30	31	1	2	3

MIDNIGHT

AQUARIUS

PISCES

ARIES

TAURUS

GEMINI

AM

CANCER

LEO

MIDDAY

VI

PM

Rows (left axis): MIDNIGHT, 1, 2, 3, 4, 5, AM 6, 7, 8, 9, 10, 11, MIDDAY 12, 1, 2, 3, 4, 5, PM 6, 7, 8, 9, 10, 11, 12

MT birth time. Where they cross is your Rising Sign. Don't forget to subtract an

6	7	8	9	10	11	12	13	14	15	16	17	18	19	20	21

0
1
2
3
4
5
6
7
8
9
10
11
12
1
2

BRA

3
4
5

SCORPIO

6
7

SAGITTARIUS

8
9

CAPRICORN

10

AQUARIUS

11
12

THE ZODIAC AT A GLANCE

Placed	Sign	Symbol	Glyph	Polarity	Element	Quality	Planet	Glyph	Metal	Stone	Opposite
1	Aries	Ram	♈	+	Fire	Cardinal	Mars	♂	Iron	Bloodstone	Libra
2	Taurus	Bull	♉	−	Earth	Fixed	Venus	♀	Copper	Sapphire	Scorpio
3	Gemini	Twins	♊	+	Air	Mutable	Mercury	☿	Mercury	Tiger's Eye	Sagittarius
4	Cancer	Crab	♋	−	Water	Cardinal	Moon	☽	Silver	Pearl	Capricorn
5	Leo	Lion	♌	+	Fire	Fixed	Sun	☉	Gold	Ruby	Aquarius
6	Virgo	Maiden	♍	−	Earth	Mutable	Mercury	☿	Mercury	Sardonyx	Pisces
7	Libra	Scales	♎	+	Air	Cardinal	Venus	♀	Copper	Sapphire	Aries
8	Scorpio	Scorpion	♏	−	Water	Fixed	Pluto	♇	Plutonium	Jasper	Taurus
9	Sagittarius	Archer	♐	+	Fire	Mutable	Jupiter	♃	Tin	Topaz	Gemini
10	Capricorn	Goat	♑	−	Earth	Cardinal	Saturn	♄	Lead	Black Onyx	Cancer
11	Aquarius	Waterbearer	♒	+	Air	Fixed	Uranus	♅	Uranium	Amethyst	Leo
12	Pisces	Fishes	♓	−	Water	Mutable	Neptune	♆	Tin	Moonstone	Virgo

THE ZODIAC, PLANETS
AND CORRESPONDENCES

In the first column of the table of correspondence, I list the signs of the Zodiac as they order themselves around their circle; starting with Aries and finishing with Pisces. In the last column, I list the signs as they will appear as opposites to those in the first column. For example, the sign which will be positioned opposite Aries, in a circular chart will be Libra.

Each sign of the Zodiac is either positive or negative. This by no means suggests that they are either 'good' or 'bad', but that they are either extrovert, outgoing, masculine signs (positive), or introspective, receptive, feminine signs (negative).

Each sign of the Zodiac will belong to one of the four Elements: Fire, Air, Earth or Water. Fire signs are creative and enthusiastic; Air signs are mentally active and thoughtful; Earth signs are constructive and practical; Water signs are emotional and have strong feelings.

Each sign of the Zodiac also belongs to one of the Qualities: Cardinal, Fixed or Mutable. Cardinal signs are initiators and pioneers; Fixed signs are consistent and inflexible; Mutable signs are educators and live to serve.

So, each sign will be either positive or negative, and will belong to one of the Elements and to one of the Qualities. You can see from the table, for example, that Aries is a positive, Cardinal, Fire sign.

The table also shows which planets rule each sign. For example, Mars is the ruling planet of Aries. Each planet represents a particular facet of personality - Mars represents physical energy and drive - and the sign which it rules is the one with which it has most in common,

The table also shows which metals and gem stones are associated with, or correspond with the signs of the Zodiac. Again, the correspondence is made when a metal or stone possesses properties that are held in common with a particular sign of the Zodiac. This system of correspondences can be extended to encompass any group, whether animal, vegetable or mineral - as well as people! For example, each sign of the Zodiac is associated with particular flowers and herbs, with particular animals, with particular towns and countries, and so on.

It is an interesting exercise when learning about astrology, to guess which sign of the Zodiac rules a particular thing, by trying to match its qualities with the appropriate sign.

The News of the Future

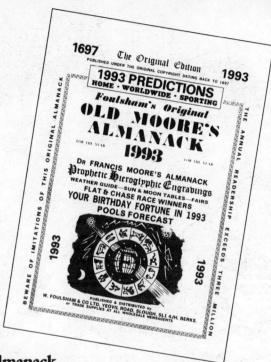

In the Almanack

Racing Tips — All the Classics. Dozens and dozens of lucky dates to follow — for Trainers and Jockeys.

Football and Greyhounds too.

Gardening Guide — Better Everything. Bigger; better; more colour. Whatever you want! Lunar planting is the key.

Fish Attack — Anglers get the upper hand and catch more fish. Dates, times and species to fish are all here.

With Key Zodiac Sign dates of course.

A great New Year investment for you.
An inexpensive, fun gift for your friends.

Look for it at W. H. Smith, John Menzies, Martins and all good newsagents.